Father; a Contribution to Social Psychology ([1963] 1969); in it, he sought explanations for a world in change. He was particularly concerned with fathers, who were increasingly disappearing from their children's life, themselves living in an anonymous "fatherless" mass society, one ruled and determined by an elite of "equals." He was aware that such "equals" were in fact nothing of the kind, though he did not mention that only men are included among the powerful "equals." Today women still play almost no significant role in the world of economic experts, multinational concerns, and politics, and hold few positions of leadership. Are fathers whose professional lives remain a mystery to their families a presence at home, in the family, at all? What is the relationship between patriarchy and matriarchy within the family, and how are the ethics that govern a family related to those of society? What problems does the present generation have with its mothers and fathers?

In several places I have tried to show that on the inside of society, that is, in the family, several typical microstructures may be discerned. The father, as the socially appointed head of the family, remains at the same time the egocentric, spoiled child of a mother who accepts or even encourages such behavior (though she also regards it with contempt). The mother, who on the one hand nurtures the father, can also be extensively dependent on him, leaning heavily on him, idealizing him, and steering clear of problems and difficulties.

The mother's varied roles stand in opposition to one another. The often overly nurturing mother feels responsible for the entire family, infantilizing all the family members (including her husband), but she herself remains childlike and depends on her husband as the "strong" one. Thus, contrasting types of behavior are often found simultaneously: On the one hand the woman unconsciously assumes the role of the omnipotent mother, but on the other hand she remains her mother's daughter or makes her husband into a mother or a father.

Women are often forced into the role of a mother whose task is to be responsible for everything. Men too find it difficult to free themselves from their dependence on the mother and can liberate themselves only with difficulty from behaving like a tyranically dependent child.

Men's striving to exclude women from their "brotherhoods" has been interpreted by psychoanalysts as an attempt to free themselves from the dependent mother-child relationship and avenge themselves on a disappointing mother. As paterfamilias, a man can satisfy both his need to be the head of the family and his regressive wishes to remain his mother's spoiled child.

Naturally one also encounters many other types of family structures, including those in which mothers and women have (like their husbands) adapted themselves to modern society, striving above all for self-realization and influence in both their careers and marriages; only a very few, however, succeed in attaining positions of leadership and penetrating into male circles. The numbers of such women have increased in the so-called age of the pill; they sometimes tend to remain childless.

Anyone who hopes to understand the present generation's difficulties with its mothers and fathers must first clarify what age he wants to assign to the "present" generation in order to be better able to make such distinctions. People who were born between 1940 and 1950 had different childhood experiences than those who were born around 1960. Today's thirty and forty year olds were influenced by the events of the Second World War and postwar circumstances in ways that twenty year olds could not have been.

Much has been written about the second generation following the Hitler era in Germany, and in particular about their conflicts with their fathers. A person who was born in 1940 often had to do without a father during the years of early childhood, and after the father returned found it difficult to get along with this stranger. Moreover, in Germany these fathers returned as broken, disappointed men whose self-esteem had been gravely called into question, and they in no way conformed to the ideal picture that their children had formed of them.

The mother, either widowed or alone during the father's long absence while at war, became the head of the family and learned to bear the sole responsibility for her children over the course of many years. When the war ended, she was no longer prepared to subordinate herself to the returning, discouraged father or to accord him the place of the spoiled child in the family again. She had usually learned to make her way in society and did not want to be forced back into the role of a woman who was utterly absorbed in her family.

An example should help to illustrate the typically problematic relationship between parents and the generation of sons born during the Second World War.

Paul was born in 1943. His father was an officer, and Paul saw him only a few times during the war. After the war, his father remained a prisoner of war in Russia for several years. Paul lived with his mother and siblings in a small village where his mother taught at the elementary school. He felt dependent upon her but had to resign himself early on to the fact that his needs to be spoiled and nurtured could be fulfilled only in limited measure. For not only did his mother have to look after three children and a household, but her work also made great demands on her.

Paul soon learned to suppress his feelings of being denied his fair share, as well as feelings of rage and fear at being left alone much of the time. He sought to master anything that disappointed him or made him afraid with the help of so-called transitional objects; that is, he exaggerated his reliance on stuffed animals for support, took them to bed to console himself, spoke to them, confided in them, and so forth. Somewhat later it was his absorption in his hobbies that alleviated his fear of being alone.

The father, who returned home from prisoner of war camp a sick and broken man, laid claim to all of the mother's attention. He could make demands that Paul never dared to make. The father became the center of attention, a spoiled and tyrannical child, a mother's boy, displacing all of the other family members to the fringes of maternal attention. Before long little was left of Paul's ideal image of his father.

The father was sick for a long time and unable to return to his former occupation, as well as probably unwilling to trouble himself with work below the level of his earlier professional activity. Thus the mother had to work harder than ever to provide for the family and had hardly any time at all left over for her children.

When the father finally recuperated sufficiently, both physically and mentally, he managed to get a well-paid job in business through connections from earlier years.

The mother stopped working and withdrew into a kind of resentful dependence on the father. In the meantime, Paul's attitude toward his father had become one of utter contempt; toward his mother he hardly had any attitude at all any more. As a child he had worshipped her, to a large extent identified with her, and had accepted (if only grudgingly) that she could not pay as much attention to him as he would have liked. Later on, he found her conduct toward the father incomprehensible and somewhat repugnant.

Paul participated in the student protests at the end of the 1960s with only moderate enthusiasm. The only thing he shared with the other students was contempt for his father's generation. Nor did he modify his reticence when he later married. The focus of his adult life were artistic and literary interests, as transitional objects and hobbies had been in his childhood. He was capable of opening up only toward his small children. He quite obviously enjoyed being both a better mother and a better father to them than he felt his own parents had been. Not until his mother began to show greater independence following the death of his father did he attempt to renew close contact with her. His search for models usually remained unsuccessful or met with only brief success, for no one could substitute for the loss of his early father image and fulfill the high ideal expectations he associated with it.

Transitional objects such as stuffed animals and other toys, and later interests such as hobbies and artistic activities, represent a kind of symbol for the comforting mother-child relationship. A kind of play space (Erikson) develops between mother and child, enabling the child to break free of an exaggerated dependence. Even in his adult years, Paul attached great importance to retaining adequate space for himself and his interests, thereby protecting himself against new dependencies. Since no so-called triad with the parents had been established in early childhood, and no basis of trust could be established with the father following his return, Oedipal conflicts with the father led finally to a complete rupture in the relationship. Even so, as a talented person capable of sublimating his conflicts, Paul succeeded in stabilizing his psychic needs through professional and artistic activity; he also did so through his role as father, which allowed him to see in himself a piece of a lost ideal.

Paul's case was not unlike the life history of a patient born somewhat later.

Karl began psychotherapeutic treatment for loneliness and depression. He had first met his father when he was about seven years old. Up until then his mother had worked and cared for her two children by herself. Karl had frequent psychosomatic illnesses; from all of this one might conclude that he had not been able to fully accomplish the necessary separation from an overly close relationship to the mother of early childhood.

The father, returning as a fallen hero, utterly failed to understand his son's negative attitude. He responded with rather callous punishments. The upshot was that relatively early on Karl severed his relationship with his father once and for all. Even as an adult he habitually reacted with psychosomatic symptoms whenever he had reason to feel lonely or alienated or oppressed by guilt. Nor had he enjoyed the benefits of a triadic relationship among father, mother, and son. He hated his father, but above all he feared him.

Karl became heavily involved in the student movement during the late 1960s. His relationships with women were complicated. Though he longed for intimacy with them, he was at the same time afraid of becoming too involved. He was also capable of sublimation and withdrew into scholarly and artistic activities in order to avoid both his separation anxieties and fear of becoming involved.

Since he had a high ego ideal (that is, he made great moral demands on himself and others), he often despised not only his own father (who was occasionally unscrupulous and whom Karl regarded as deceitful) but many other fathers whom he met during the course of his life. At the same time, Karl was himself in danger of becoming an offender; for owing to his lack of identification with his father, he had not formed a limit-setting superego or conscience that might have held his struggle against a deidealized world of fathers within bounds. He often came close to joining a terrorist cell; it was only his loathing for all forms of violence that prevented him from doing so. This abhorrence was also rooted in the fact that his father had expressed his frustration with his son in a somewhat sadistic fashion, habitually beating him severely. Often, it seems to me, such a combination of a high ego ideal and a lack of identification with the strictures of a respected and loved father (that is, the lack of a binding superego) has led young people to become involved in terrorist associations.

Another case history, that of a woman named Anne, had clear "female" features despite many similarities to the experiences of the young men portrayed above.

Anne was also born during the Second World War; her father too was a soldier, and she rarely saw him. Her memories of him were positive; she felt herself recognized and loved by him during the brief moments they shared.

When he was reported missing at the end of the war, she was for a long time unable to accept that he was probably dead and would not return to his family. Anne secretly blamed her mother, believing that she had not treated him lovingly enough. On the other hand, Anne loved and admired her mother because she had taken over the father's business and provided for the family by herself.

Anne, like Paul and Karl, struggled with wishes for dependence that could not be adequately fulfilled and that called forth intense feelings of ambivalence toward her mother. But Anne defended herself against her feelings of hatred that coexisted with love, for ultimately her link with her mother was Anne's most important personal relationship, and the child could not forego the nurture she received from it. She struggled for a long time to retain her mother's love and at the same time her own independence.

Prior to her activity in the women's movement, Anne became involved in the student movement; during this period she entered into relationships with several men. Basically she did not trust anyone and was convinced that she had been abandoned. This had to do not only with the early interruption in her relationship with her father but above all with her relationship with her mother, whose conduct toward Anne had been quite inconsistent.

If Anne later participated actively in the women's movement, she did so not only out of identification with a virtuous mother who had been forced to make her own way against great adversity in a man's world but also in order to make herself less dependent on her mother and her mother's nurture. Anne learned to love other women, which was a great relief to her, for her feelings of animosity toward her mother had called forth feelings of guilt and anxiety, and triggered depressions.

In the women's movement, Anne was able to engage in open and intense discussions with women without becoming overly dependent on them. She had finally succeeded in learning to love women, she said. Prior to her marriage, she had a lesbian relationship, which despite some conflicts was satisfying.

This sketch of one woman's life is meant simply to clarify how an exaggerated dependence on the mother can frequently trigger a psychic struggle around the relationship with the mother, particularly in the absence of a father or of sufficient attention from him. Such conflicts can lead to depression and deep-rooted feelings of insecurity. There were doubtless many causes, both social and personal, for the intensification of the women's movement during the 1960s—but a number of women who were especially active had suffered a fate similar to Anne's.

Today the women's movement is at a crossroads. Will it become bogged down in a wave of nostalgic longing for a "new femininity," as already happened once during the 1950s? Or has a state of critical awareness become sufficiently stabilized so that there is no more going back? Disappointment with unfatherly fathers can sometimes be so great that a woman prefers to push forward toward autonomy and self-realization rather than retreat into a disappointing dependency.

People have argued time and again about whether the psychic structure of women has changed over the course of time. There are debates about whether their egos have become stronger, allowing them to be guided by their own judgments, and thus no longer fitting the picture of women that was sketched by Freud (that of a woman ruled by her emotions and regressive needs and not by objective or moral considerations). It is obvious that in our time, after men have forced them into participation during the last two World Wars, women will not allow themselves to be completely driven from "men's affairs" again. But today it is not merely external forces that drive them toward autonomy but their own critical awareness and desire for a more meaningful kind of life.

The word *partnership* will cause many readers to think not of business partnerships, group associations, or relationships between people of the same sex but rather of marital or marriagelike relationships between two people of the opposite sex. The following prognosis for the future of partnership will thus also be confined to this sense of the word. Perhaps one might just as well ask: "Does marriage, does the enduring relationship between a man and a woman have a future, or will such relationships between two people be possible only on a short-term basis?" People have in truth been concerned about this question for centuries; yet today it is more immediate than ever.

Viewed from a historical perspective, marriages for love have existed for only a short while. For millennia, the institution of marriage was based on male ownership rights over women. In the list presented in the Sixth Commandment, women in no way occupied the first place but came after the house. Until well into the bourgeois era, the patriarchally ruled kinship system determined who was to marry whom. Yet compared to circumstances in, say, India, paradisiacal circumstances prevailed in Europe and North America. Today marriages of inclination have become a fixture in our society, and men and women enjoy the right of individual choice. Adultery, which has always been permitted to men, either officially or unofficially, meant physical or social destruction to women for centuries; now it no longer triggers dramatic reactions from us. For some time now, adultery has been a socially recognized common law—naturally even more so for men than for women.

Much has changed. Christian concepts of love and faithfulness play only a minor role nowadays. But is there greater partnership between men and women as a result? Can both claim the same rights? Is a man as bound to a woman as she is to him? Does he assume the same responsibility for the children? Is he obligated to show the same degree of empathy for his partner, or to observe the same constancy? Are not women still the victims of a presupposition of male superiority, even in sexual matters? When our era's male ideal of productivity is extended into the area of sexuality, there is the danger that women will accommodate themselves to this ideal, believing that because of the pill they must always be sexually available in order to be regarded as capable of performing.

Women are certainly inclined to critical self-perception, far more than men, but they frequently tend to look at themselves with a man's eyes in so doing, accepting his judgments and prejudices about the nature, tasks, and worth of a woman. Despite women's sexual freedom, they are still bound by male concepts and notions of value and judge themselves to a large extent according to the male criterion of dutiful, attractive feminity.

Can anything resembling true partnership develop under such conditions? The assumption of male superiority still lurking in women's minds must first be brought to consciousness. Not until women learn to think more critically than in the past and free their self-perception from male notions about women will the preconditions for true partnership between man and woman have been created.

This certainly does not mean that women should become like men. It means that they should give thought to themselves and their own judgments and emotional capabilities. For despite greater professional independence, despite sexual freedom, and despite critical feminist insights, young women today are still tied to a model of life in which marriage or a marriagelike relationship provides the focus and meaning of life. Since this central desire, giving meaning to a person's life, is closely tied to notions of beauty, youth, and fertility, older women as a rule experience themselves as worthless once their children no longer need them, and they believe that they can no longer live up to male notions of sexual attractiveness.

To be sure, men also long for a loving partnership founded on mutual understanding, but they are taught from the beginning of life that the capacity for separation is a necessary male virtue. Separation from the mother (and later from a close relationship with a woman) is something that they, like society, regard as necessary in order to develop themselves further as men and attain masculine "maturity." For women, on the other hand, the ability to form bonds and relationships is seen as the supreme value. Women continue to regard the relationship between the sexes as the meaning of their life.

With such different evaluations of what constitutes people's worth or the meaning of their life, men and women will not be able to agree on the form and content of a partnership. Both men and women will continue to deceive themselves. Only when both become conscious of their uncritical, gender-specific prejudices, their difficulties in understanding, and their painful entanglements will they be able to achieve something resembling real partnership and equality.

7

Must We Hate
Our Mothers?

IN RECENT YEARS, the women's movement has devoted much attention to the relationship between mother and daughter. In such discussions, mothers are repeatedly characterized as an obstacle to their daughter's emancipation. Mothers, it is said, refuse to release their daughters from dependence or permit them disposition of their own bodies and sexuality (which daughters can thus experience only with a guilty conscience or in a self-sacrificing manner). Hence a mother impedes her daughter's development toward self-sufficiency: A daughter cannot separate herself from her mother because she is not permitted to abandon her early childhood dependence without suffering guilt and fear of rejection.

Such ideas depict mothers as the principal villains in their children's faulty development and imply that the emancipation of women is hindered even more strongly by mothers than by a male-dominated society. Even in the theories of many psychoanalysts (Chasseguet-Smirgel, Horney, Klein, Zilboorg, and others) women's so-called man-hating represents merely a defense against an original hatred of an omnipotent mother who refused to release her daughter from dependence and prohibited the small girl from autonomous gratification (i.e., masturbation). For these theorists, all hatred, whether of women toward men or of men toward women, is ultimately nothing more than hatred toward the mother and her power over the helpless child. No consideration is given to social values, conscious and unconscious fantasies, gender-specific child rearing, or later influences and emotional wounds. This reductive tendency, in which the mother is branded as the source of all ills, stifles thought and impedes analysis of the diversity of influences on human behavior in general, and of the development of women in particular.

Many mothers also feel drawn to the women's movement, hoping there to find understanding of their difficulties. But as a result of the negative attitudes described above, they feel like second-class citizens and are once again left to deal with their problems on their own. A mother who receives no help in her self-emancipation remains isolated. She can only raise her children as she herself was brought up; that is, she forces her daughters into the same role patterns that were prescribed for her.

Thus one wonders why such mother-blaming attitudes could have made such an impression on many women. For mothers too are women, and as women subject to the same fate should have the right to the same understanding from members of their own sex.

In order to better understand the situation between mothers and daughters, it is necessary to make the distinction between a mother's *psychic* reality and her *external* reality. In other words: Although a mother is very powerful in the fantasy life and experience of her children, since they are dependent on her, she is still largely powerless with respect to her position in the family and society. Thus mothers frequently attempt in vain to protect their children from the father's callousness and lack of understanding, and later from authority figures in school and society. Against her better judgment, a mother must encourage her children to adapt to an environment that is often hostile to children. As a rule, people do not recognize just how laborious (and frequently hopeless) a mother's efforts are as she attempts to prevail against her environment in order to spare her children greater wounds. Maternal protection of the child can never be complete; it is small wonder that mothers constrain their children to conform in deference to their own and their children's weaknesses. But these very constraints are often the cause of many children's rejection or even hate of their mothers, when their own self-sufficiency grows. One finds this rejection and hatred in both sexes, not only in daughters. Children especially resent the powerlessness of their mothers in the external world because the mother appears in a child's eyes (that is, in its psychic reality), as powerful or even omnipotent, depending on the degree of the child's dependence.

The revitalization of the women's movement during the 1960s and 1970s also revived discussions within psychoanalytic circles about the theory of female development. Psychoanalysis has met with resistance from many feminists. Although this rejection of psychoanalysis is based on partly justified criticism of psychoanalytic notions of femininity, it also has to do with a denial of unconscious psychic processes within the women's movement that frequently persists in a purely rational (and, in consequence, superficial) discussion of the psychology of women. Whether one wants to acknowledge it or not, the simple truth is that early-childhood fantasies and childhood identifications and drive developments do have a profound influence on a woman's later behavior. Repressed childhood fantasies of a mother's omnipotence do persist unconsciously into adult life, producing anxiety, lack of self-sufficiency, and hatred.

Freud made the pathbreaking discovery that it is not only external events and experiences that leave their mark on the human psyche; fantasy can give new interpretations to external events, thus creating a new psychic reality that, in turn, can influence external reality and thereby help to shape it. Thus fantasies help to mold a daughter's relationship with her mother, which is based only in part on the mother's actual conduct. It is therefore important to understand more precisely the mixture of objective events and the way they are subjectively experienced in the psyche. A daughter either overlooks her mother's objective behavior and powerlessness or even misconstrues it as its opposite. Unless we undertake the laborious task of working through customary misunderstandings between mother and daughter and making their origins conscious, we will not be able to even understand, let alone improve, this relationship, unique and crucial as it is to a woman's development.

When child rearing becomes the sole responsibility of the mother during the years of early childhood, or when the mother herself depends on her unique importance to the child, the child frequently has the feeling of being clung to and ruled by her. In a society in which the small family plays a central role, in which a mother must suffer guilt if she has a career and leaves her child in the care of other women or of day-care centers, and in which the father does not take part in the early years of child rearing—in such a society a daughter's heightened dependence on her mother will be difficult to outgrow with age. The consequence to the daughter is that long-lasting lack of self-sufficiency of which everyone complains and feelings of hatred toward the mother. Moreover, owing to prevailing value norms, a daughter is expected to identify with her mother and her mother's forms of behavior; in contrast, a son is urged to free himself from his overly dependent relationship with his mother relatively early. A boy later tends to deny and repress feelings more than a girl, however; his self-sufficiency is largely the product of a defense against more intimate relationships with others.

Though the relationship between mother and daughter is so often characterized as disastrous, we must not overlook the fact that the relationship between mother and son can also be marked by intense hostility. As long as the mother is solely responsible for raising the infant, the child will inevitably develop an exaggerated dependence on her, which she in turn can exploit, producing hatred as a result. Hatred toward a mother who is experienced as omnipotent, in turn triggers feelings of anxiety and guilt.

A boy often abandons his identification with the mother too early, thus disrupting his maturation in the emotional realm. But in a boy this can lead to an even greater underlying dependence on the mother than in a girl. For internalization of maternal roles and behavior can contribute to a child's independence; step by step the child learns to satisfy its needs itself and to allay its own fears.

The right of an infant to cling to its love objects during the various stages of its development should be taken just as seriously as the right of older children and adolescents to detach themselves from the mother and family. A child's right to an appropriate measure of autoerotic gratification should also be respected. Mothers tend to permit this to boys more than girls. Psychoanalysts have pointed out that prohibition of pleasure in one's own body can stir up animosity toward the mother. In consequence, feelings of anxiety and renewed clinging tendencies appear, for the child fears that the mother will reject it in retaliation for its hatred.

That mothers take a negative attitude toward the sexuality of their daughters, as the latter often complain, is surely not just a product of their daughters' imagination. This negative stance has its roots in the mother's own fears, stemming from her own early childhood. But daughters may also fantasize maternal prohibitions because they are directing their own sexuality away from the mother and toward the father. Prohibitions that the daughter produces in fantasy may derive from an insurmountable, exaggerated dependence on the mother. In such cases, impulses toward self-sufficiency, above all of a sexual nature, can produce unbearable anxiety; prohibitions then have an anxiety-*alleviating* effect.

Many mothers tend to see their daughters, more than their sons, as a part of themselves, so that they are unable to fully appreciate their daughters' particular character and individual needs. But a mother may also unconsciously perceive in her daughter rejected parts of her own self, which she then combats in her daughter.

The more clearly psychoanalysis came to recognize the extent to which upbringing, fantasy, and even parents' values influence the psychosexual development of the child, the more the importance of relationships with other people came to be the focal point of psychoanalytic interest. Particular attention has been devoted to the work of Margaret Mahler, whose observations were made over the course of many years and became the basis for her theories about the stepwise separation and individuation of human beings. As mentioned, Mahler's research has established that a child's development is dependent on the ability of the parent to adequately acknowledge the degree of self-sufficiency appropriate to the child's age.

In order to be able to separate itself from the mother, a child needs to have possibilities for relationships with people other than the mother by the end of the second year of life at the latest. As a rule, this opportunity is presented by the father, whose participation in the child rearing can never come too early if the child is to attain the necessary self-sufficiency and inner security. The individuation process can only succeed when both the father and the mother treat the child with empathy, so that the child may at times experience the father as a bridge to the mother.

Centuries-old practices of child rearing in our society make it difficult for both parents to treat each other with mutual respect and to approach each other empathetically and without prejudice. Each parent must be capable of empathetic relationships with more than one person at the same time in order to be able to understand the child and its conflicting needs.

I would like to offer an example of the sort of childhood

experience that can lead to a more or less final turning away from the mother.

Martha consulted me because she was suffering from frigidity and a diminished sense of self-esteem. She had been a student for many years but had never attained a degree. When she became pregnant, she married; both marriage and the child came, for her, at a good time. They meant an interruption of her burdensome studies at the university. Moreover, the child provided the proof she had hoped for of her womanhood. She had long secretly doubted her sexual identity, feeling her body to be inferior and like a boy's.

Her sexual relations with her husband were poor; she endured them only with effort. Nor did marriage and motherhood do anything to change this. She felt empty, unfulfilled, and once again resumed her studies. On the recommendation of a group of women with whom she discussed her problems, she entered into sexual relationships with other men. In so doing she primarily sought men who could play the role of father in her emotional life.

As far as she could remember, her childhood had been quite happy during her first four years. Her father was away at the war, and her mother lived in a small city with relatives. Since the mother could no more tolerate her daughter's outbreaks of defiance than her daughter could tolerate her mother's withdrawal of love, Martha soon acquiesced and became a well-behaved child, and was particularly dependent on her mother.

All of this changed dramatically when the father returned from the war. The mother became wholly engrossed in the father, just as previously she had been with her daughter. Soon Martha's mother was again pregnant and she gave birth to a son; Martha was five years old at the time. Filled with painful disappointment and rage, Martha turned away from her mother and sought consolation from her father, whom her mother so revered. But he was clearly unable to recognize his daughter's need to establish a productive relationship with another person in order to free herself from dependence on the mother and alleviate her hatred toward her. He reacted hypersensitively, rejecting her infantile-sexual affections. The mother answered her daughter's withdrawal by withholding love. As a child, Martha was often able to observe her parents' lovemaking, for she slept in their bedroom until she was thirteen. She herself was forbidden to masturbate, so she felt hopelessly at the mercy of her sexual arousal.

Disappointed by both parents, but also incapable of autonomy, Martha thus remained dependent on her parents' values. During puberty, with its renewed conflicts associated with the drives and with dependence, she again felt abandoned by her mother and rejected as a woman by her father. When Martha returned home late, her parents accused her of being a slut and threatened to throw her out. Again and again she attempted to improve her feeling of self-esteem through sexual relationships with men. These attempts did not meet with success, however, for men showed her no more understanding and respect than her parents had.

In the course of her marriage she made her husband into her mother: She could not live without him, and was as dependent on him as a child upon its mother, but set little store in her sexual relations with him. She forced her husband into the role of housewife, at the same time despising him for acquiescing. Because of her animosity and disappointment, as well as her failure to achieve age-appropriate separation from her mother, her early identifi-

In our society, women at this age are often burdened by their roles as housewives and mothers. They are generally expected to be content with their lot, to resign themselves to the fact that their children are becoming older and need their mothers less, and to the fact that their husbands are inclined to look for other partners. If they wish to resume a professional career, they will encounter great difficulty in finding a job, as is widely recognized.

In *Passages* (1974), her book on the mid-life crisis, Gail Sheehy has written of the possibilities for inner change and development in women too during this stage of life. According to Sheehy, a necessary prerequisite would be the surmounting of previous superego restrictions. It seems to me that Sheehy is propagating a somewhat frantic notion of self-realization, one that owes a great deal to ideals of productivity in our society. In general, it is possible to fulfill such ideals only when other family members, in addition to the mother, share in caring for the children. But surely only a small percentage of women enjoy the benefit of such circumstances.

Social role expectations are becoming more and more fluid. Women are even more strongly plagued than men by feelings of insecurity. Contradictory demands are made: Our society increasingly expects and insists that women make themselves independent. At the same time, women are unable to avail themselves of potential new freedoms, for they lack the necessary familial, professional, and psychological preconditions. In consequence, many women suffer from increasing feelings of worthlessness. They are supposed to be mothers who can empathize with the complicated psychological problems of their children, comport themselves as good housewives, and, in addition, be equal partners for their husbands. They are expected to succeed professionally as well. These are demands that few indeed are capable of fulfilling.

Precisely because people today encounter fewer conventional social expectations, disoriented adults long to be able to anticipate what sort of behavior they may expect from themselves and others, and for advance knowledge of how they can resolve the internal crises of mid-life and the partner problems that accompany them. Thus the temptation to turn to psychology for pat answers to such quandaries is considerable.

Certainly people of different ages are confronted with a variety of questions and problems that call for answers and solutions specifically relevant to people of their age. But we also know that the manner in which crises at a given age are handled depends upon how a person has thus far attempted to solve previous problems and conflicts. From the very beginning of life, we all have to survive various developmental and transition phases, each of which presents its own crises. Thus it would be a mistake to forget the past and deny its significance for present conduct when dealing with adults. A new beginning at the so-called mid-life point is possible only when a person attempts to understand and integrate the past.

A great deal of psychoanalytic research has been devoted to the various phases of childhood and adolescence and to typical developmental events in infancy; the adult stage has, in contrast, been largely neglected or regarded as simply a repetition of childhood conflicts.

Many studies leave open the question of how mid-life crises might affect women who, though emotionally capable of becoming independent, have great difficulty in doing so as a result of their social, economic, and familial circumstances.

In studies of patients between thirty-five and sixty years of age at the Sigmund Freud Institute in Frankfurt, we found it difficult to view the problems of this phase of life independently from earlier developmental stages and their conflicts. Just as puberty is influenced by the way in which the Oedipal conflict has been solved, the Oedipal conflict is in turn dependent on the course of the separation-individuation process that occurs during the second year of life. Even if all later conflict situations do reflect, to an extent, problems similar to bonding wishes and needs for autonomy, they still take place on a different plane of ego development and in other life situations with new contents and conflicts—ones that play no role at all in childhood. Thus the older they become, the more people must confront death; they develop a new sense of time and of self. The changes that accompany this are even more far-reaching for women than for men. Women must endure and work through the fading of sexual attractiveness and the object relations it determines, as well as of the possibility of bearing children. In addition, there are new separations to master; this is possible only when one has developed the ability to be alone.

In every phase of life, the destinies of men and women are distinct, at least in our society. This does not mean that we are dealing here with purely biologically determined developments that rest on the anatomical difference between the sexes, or with developments that can be traced back to innate psychological qualities. Simone de Beauvoir ([1949] 1953) rightly observed that a person is not born a woman but made into one; that is, social prejudices determine what a woman should become. A girl's up-bringing is still considerably different from a boy's; the expectations, hopes, limitations, and role prescriptions laid upon women by society are fundamentally different from those to which men must conform.

The ideal of self-realization promoted by our culture for both men and women thus frequently stands in glaring contrast to a woman's internal and external possibilities.

Women are confronted with the problems of mid-life even before the fortieth year of life. They must learn to live with the fact that their children no longer need them and that, in most cases, they can no longer gain a foothold in professional life. To develop internal autonomy in this situation, to avoid being overcome by feelings of worth-lessness and uselessness often seems a hopeless proposi-tion.

At mid-life many women must also come to terms with the fact that their heterosexual relationships have not been satisfying to them. Often they feel guilty as a result and attempt to punish themselves for their inability to expe-rience orgasm by behaving masochistically and submis-sively toward their husbands. They may attribute what they interpret as their own inability to love to an under-lying hatred of men. Often they believe they must pay sexually for what they feel is their inability to be alone or to take control of their own lives. But sexuality experi-enced in this way produces only fresh feelings of hatred that in turn provoke yet more masochistically submissive behavior, intensifying feelings of worthlessness.

I would like now to attempt to show how crises can become manifest in various phases of life and how such crises are linked to one another.

Helene, a woman about forty, sought treatment because she suffered from depression. For many years she had been involved in an intense relationship with a married man who could not make up his mind to separate from his wife. Helene had her own career and was in fact quite successful, although she felt that she was not able to hold her own. She had always suffered from feelings of worthlessness. She had experienced a number of crises during both puberty and adulthood; these centered principally around the conflicts between individuation and childhood dependence, between love and hate, and the guilt associated with them.

Psychoanalysts assign two causes to the fact that women in general are unable to develop an adequate feeling of self-esteem and are thus overly at the mercy of a narcissistic need to be loved: First, a mother's lack of love (or ambivalent love) for her daughter; second, a feeling of physical inferiority that has never been surmounted. Frequently people overlook the fact that both are the result of upbringing and the socially higher value placed on masculinity. In Helene the disruption of self-esteem had come about as follows:

For a long time she persisted in an overly dependent relationship with her mother. Attempts at age-appropriate separation from her mother had provoked more intense feelings than usual. She had little communication with her brother, who was two years older. Her brother was jealous of her and saw her as their mother's favorite child. The mother was typical for our society, inasmuch as in principle she accorded men far greater prestige than women with respect to matters of intelligence and social influence. Thus she submitted to the tyranny of both husband and son, who were themselves unaware of the extent to which they had each remained dependent on their mother. For this they were secretly ridiculed by mother and daughter. In fact, in this family both sexes shared a rather similar disdain for the other sex.

As a result of these feelings, a relationship of trust with her father and brother that might have alleviated Helene's dependence on her mother was prevented from developing. Her mother reacted negatively to the girl's overtures toward her father; a severe taboo was placed on masturbation and sexuality. As a result, the girl had to suppress the accompanying Oedipal fantasies, and she was unable to develop a pleasurable autonomous relationship to her own body.

There were many causes for these deep wounds to Helene's sense of self-esteem. On the one hand, she had often identified with her mother, whom she herself despised for her frequently submissive behavior. On the other hand, she was more or less openly contemptuous of all things female; this attitude she derived from her father and brother but also from her mother.

Helene's emotional ambivalence toward both parents caused her severe guilt; she questioned her own worth as a person capable of loving, and as the daughter of such parents. When she later entered into similar crisis situations by becoming involved with men who were already married, it was more than an expression of an unsurmounted Oedipal conflict (and the accompanying guilt); she was expressing a wish to free herself from an exaggerated dependence on a mother imago. She did not succeed in the latter because in every intimate relationship, she repeated both the early symbiosis with the mother and the wishes for autonomy that stood in conflict with it, all of which necessarily forced her into renewed dependence and emotional ambivalence.

Only during the course of the analysis did Helene learn

to tolerate her ambivalent feelings more adequately and bear her guilt feelings. This encouraged her autonomy, and with it the positive side of her relationship to her mother. Love now took precedence over hate, so that her mother representation increasingly took on the quality of a "good internalization." A "bad internalization," that is the internalization of an object at which rage, vengeance, and denigration are directed—and from whom separation has taken place—prevents the broadening of the ego and the consequent maturing of the person through new and varied identifications. The consequence is frequently a lasting attitude of reproach accompanied by ungratified feelings of dependence and self-hatred. Under such circumstances, potentials that are the basis for age-appropriate autonomy remain undeveloped.

Perhaps in our society we do not really become adults until mid-life, if at all. According to some psychoanalytic reports (Martha Wolfenstein 1951, for example), the psychological work associated with mourning does not become possible until after puberty. It often appears as if the separation from childhood bonds or the integration of lost objects is not really completed until mid-life. If, by that time, old bonds that are carried over into the relationship with the partner cannot be given up and the lost objects freed from an excess of ambivalence and internalized, the chances for a creative use of the second half of life are slim.

The years prior to and during mid-life appear to us as a time when identifications must be integrated in order to allow for undeveloped or suppressed potentials to be realized or for new ones to be developed. But we often witness the reverse—people granting their sexual partners that which they have not been able to experience themselves. The sexual partner is thus idealized, but at the same time envy may cause this idealization to revert to denigration. Envy often prevents a person from being able to accomplish internalizations and integrate them intact. Both sexes have the tendency to exclude the other sex from their own world. Women are excluded from a professional world regarded as the domain of men; and men are excluded from the world of the family, the house, and female and maternal roles. Problems of envy are often concealed behind all of this—something that many psychoanalytic authors have overlooked. Such envy prevents both female and male partners from discovering and developing in their emotional relationships parts of themselves and potentials that they see in the other person.

The solution to these conflicts is of varying difficulty in the two sexes. The man can often bring his maternal identifications into the family if he does not defend himself against the fulfillment of such wishes because of role prejudices. Many women would be only too happy to accept such a transformation of attitude in a man, and relieved to be able to share the responsibility of child rearing. But it is far more difficult for a woman to hold her own professionally. She has to reckon with the resistance not only of her husband but of the entire social system as well.

The so-called narcissistic neuroses are at the center of theoretical interest for many psychoanalysts today. When reading authors who concern themselves with narcissistic developmental disturbances, one notices that such disturbances are discussed far more often with respect to men than women. The reasons are probably similar to those we have already encountered: what is considered to be a fundamental condition for the development of a healthy narcissism—namely the unqualified admiration of a child by its mother—is granted exclusively to boys by psychoanalytic theory and by many of our contemporaries.

If what the American psychoanalyst Heinz Kohut ([1973] 1985) considers as proven is correct—namely that the admiration of a child by its mother is necessary for the development of a healthy sense of self-esteem and for the integration of psychic structures into an independent, cohesive self—then women will always suffer from a lack of a sense of self-esteem.

Psychoanalytic theories about women are self-contradictory, however: On the one hand, women are said to be particularly narcissistic because they have been unable to develop a healthy sense of self-esteem as a result of early childhood injuries (described above). On the other hand, it is considered obvious that a woman can empathize with the child as no other family member can. The damage caused by a lack of maternal capacity for empathy has been portrayed vividly enough in the psychoanalytic literature. But how is a woman supposed to be capable of all that is demanded of a mother nowadays in the way of love and empathy when, as is stipulated by psychoanalytic theory, she herself has never enjoyed love free from ambivalence? Empathy in the mother-child relationship is rightly considered essential for the further development of the child, but the burden of guilt that is placed on a mother in this way is oppressive. We thus find here both exaggerated expectations of mothers and idealization of them.

It has often been pointed out that the tendency toward

debasement of women represents a defense against early-childhood dependence on a mother who is experienced as omnipotent. Thus fixation on the notion of a "typically" female narcissism may often be a projection of a male inability to love. A woman who, before and during mid-life, feels herself overburdened by her roles as mother and partner, and hence suffers from guilt at not being able to better cope, who has no chance of self-realization in her career, and who can count on little understanding in her struggles to achieve self-respect—such a woman will have difficulty in becoming her own mistress or "her own woman." She will find it next to impossible to build adequate self-assurance and autonomy. It is therefore not surprising that women suffer from depressive reactions more frequently than do men. Professionally, women have been and still are able to achieve self-realization only with difficulty if at the same time their dream of a great love and a family is to be fulfilled. Though this dilemma is by now a familiar one, people devote little attention to the grave problems with which women with such ideals are confronted during mid-life. In contrast, it is taken for granted that a woman will not only be able to empathize fully with the needs of her children and her husband and be happy to do so, but will be able to release her children from dependence on her without further ado once they have matured. Similarly, she is supposed to submit to her husband's needs for freedom without suffering melancholic depression.

In reality, such a thing as the fulfillment by a "great love" exists only for a short time—which is not to deny that some couples feel strong psychosexual attraction to one another and preserve it intact into old age; such a thing is possible, though rare. Even so, we all know how much mental and emotional work must be accomplished in order to maintain the vitality of a human relationship throughout the various phases of life, how much mourning (that is, the working through of loss) must be experienced in order to make possible changed attitudes and new insights.

In *A Model Childhood* ([1976] 1980), Christa Wolf has written of how feelings that one has had to deny oneself can take their vengeance. Loss of intimate memories is said to accompany the loss of memory of feelings. With this, one loses access to one's self, to which one becomes a stranger. But the inability to separate oneself from old feelings, ideals, and relationships also has grave consequences. Obstinate clinging to attitudes from the first half of life often leads to loneliness and bitterness in the second, as shown in the following example.

I had several conversations with Louise, a woman about fifty-five, who came to me at her daughter's urgent request. Louise had married shortly before the war and gave birth to two children in the ensuing years. She was a physician and continued to work except for a few brief interruptions. Her husband was her "great love" and her ideal. Her children were regarded as the fulfillment of this relationship, which was the center of her life.

When her husband returned from the war, he apparently felt cramped and confined, rather than delighted, by this idealization of himself and the marital relationship. In any case, he soon found other girlfriends, and only a few years passed before he expressed the desire for a separation. For Louise this was the biggest shock of her life; she reacted by stubbornly clinging to the marriage. To her there was only this one man, for whom, in her opinion, she was the only suitable woman.

When Louise's husband moved out of the house, she did everything in her power to bring him back. The children were fully drawn into this struggle for the father, and they came to feel that their only importance to the mother was as a link to the father. Despite her career, Louise could not free herself from her tie to her husband; she remained pathologically fixated on him and was for many years unwilling to obtain a divorce. This interfered with her own life, but especially with her relationship to her children and other people.

This obstinate posture did not change even when Louise reached mid-life. Growing older did little to change her feelings and life-style. She continued to regard her husband as the "great love of her life," to a great extent repressing her rage at him for leaving her, or preserving it only to the extent of using every means at her disposal to make separating from her impossible for him.

Louise's daughter had suffered her whole life from being drawn into her mother's pathological fixation on her father; as a result, she felt herself to be neither understood nor loved for herself. Louise was incapable of transformation or of mourning. She remained fixated on a social preconception of the "one great love" as the meaning and goal of her life. The result was that she not only completely destroyed her relationship with her husband but was also unable to feel a sense of satisfaction in her career. Moreover, she lost the love of her children. For the children of course discovered that she had no real relationship to them, nor any concern with their interests. To be sure, they felt responsible for their mother, but inwardly they largely separated themselves from her. As a result, Louise had a lonely old age. Her stubborn inner fixation on a fantasized relationship to her husband slowly but inexorably destroyed all vital contact with the people around her.

If I have associated mid-life with mourning, the purpose is to show that this phase has (and must have) something to do with the psychic processing of loss and separation if our souls are not to stagnate and loneliness is not to rule our lives, as was the case with Louise.

Part of the misery of our culture can be traced back to the cult of youth and a resistance to all that comes with age (diminishment of strength and beauty, for example). Such attitudes make us ever more susceptible to the compulsion to achieve and to compete that has taken hold of all areas of life, including sexuality.

We struggle desperately to hold off the old age that slowly draws nearer at the beginning of the second half of life; the result is that all differences between the generations are erased, with the result that they cannot complement one another in their experiences and needs and cannot learn from one another. Thus when old age is so thoroughly denigrated, as it is in a culture like ours, the second half of life cannot become a phase of maturation for the person who is aging; nor can it offer possibilities for orientation to a younger person. One would think that it would be of greater importance to elderly people to be able to pass on to the next generation their more extensive experience, their greater equanimity with respect to success or the need for recognition, and so forth; this would help people of the younger generation to be able to prepare themselves for growing old, for mid-life, and finally for death. Growing up, for all people, means a gradual leave-taking from feelings and ties with which one has previously lived. This does not mean that growing up is necessarily accompanied by the loss of a relationship; frequently it is only a matter of transforming internal and external situations within oneself or involving both one's self and others.

Mid-life is a transitional phase, one that makes particularly hard demands on women with regard to emotional readjustments. Women are habitually told that emotional relationships with other people are their life's purpose; however, changes in such relationships are unavoidable in mid-life. Often, women are unable to pursue a career and be successful until after they have separated themselves from emotional ties of a familial nature. Most people are astounded when women begin new career training at an advanced age or resume a profession they pursued earlier.

Mourning is thus a gradual working through and learning to bear losses and is a process that offers the possibility of gaining maturity through these experiences—that is, of being able to give up or transform emotional ties that no longer suit one's age or time. Being less narcissistically oriented toward success and "self-realization" goes along with this as well. This is not to disparage self-realization, which can be achieved precisely through mourning and by giving up some things during and after mid-life. But only when our culture slowly abandons its desperate youth worship and those over forty reconcile themselves to their age and the problems that accompany it, and are able to achieve a new awareness of life, will there (in my opinion) be a possibility for less of the destructiveness caused by excessive rivalry, and less of the depression caused by self-denigration. More time given to reflection in our daily lives would doubtless contribute considerably to what people nowadays call the "quality of life."

Mourning may be distinguished from melancholia inasmuch as the loss of self-esteem that characterizes melancholia is usually absent in mourning. Mourning for a lost love object, for lost happiness—whether in a sexual relationship or in a relationship to a child—can occasionally be accompanied by feelings of emptiness, lack of direction, and meaninglessness; but it is still a temporary condition. Mourning is often accompanied by a feeling of regret, for example at not having done enough, while it was still possible and necessary, for a person whom one has loved. In spite of all such forms of self-reproach, mourning is not a condition of lasting self-denigration. Even mourning over the loss of ideals does not necessarily lead to melancholia. Unlike mourning, melancholia represents a lasting condition in which there is a resurgence of feelings of anxious emptiness, of meaninglessness and worthlessness.

At mid-life and afterward, people must face the fact that it is too late to remedy some things. Often a person has placed too much emphasis on self-assertiveness and success, forgetting close ones. Children have outgrown their close relationship with their parents, and whatever they once needed but did not receive can no longer be given to them. In my experience, women generally give themselves over to such mourning more intensively than men. Men usually use the psychic mechanisms of defense, for example, those of denial and repression, more successfully than women. This also has to do with the fact that their lives are often more strongly molded by their profession, their ambitions, and their social position than by emotional relationships to fellow family members.

Does a woman at mid-life have the possibility of deciding her own fate? For the average woman in our society, whose life centers around family and children, this is rarely the case. In matters of career, she must already have decided; otherwise she will have to be content with the limited professional circumstances and opportunities available to women who have thus far devoted most of their energies to their families. In most cases she must therefore learn first and foremost to content herself with her lot during mid-life. This too is inevitably accompanied by a process of mourning, if not depression. If one learns during this time to slowly abandon false hopes and overly dependent relationships, the process can be thoroughly productive. A woman then knows that she is largely left to her own devices, is slowly approaching the end of life, and must find out for herself what she intends to make of all this. In many cases this means liberation from socially constricting preconceptions, for example about how a woman ought to look at life.

In his book *The Seasons of a Man's Life* (1978), Daniel Levinson speaks of how a man at mid-life must be in a position to no longer need "mentors," that is guiding figures, but to furnish a model and orientation for others. How can these ideas be applied to women? Have not women, in their role as mothers, always been "mentors" already? In our society this should probably be answered yes and no. To be sure, a woman is an early model for both male and female children, and in the beginning, boys as well as girls identify with her. But both sexes outgrow this dyadic relationship to her only with difficulty; for the children, she is not distanced enough, not enough of a third party around whom they can orient themselves. Instead she becomes a part of themselves, as her roles and characteristics are internalized.

But the father, too, only rarely plays the role of a mentor nowadays in our "fatherless society" (A. Mitscherlich 1963). His unknown job, his erosion through ambition and career, and the resultant inadequate affective bonding to his children only rarely allow him to become their "mentors."

Even so, mothers and fathers generally do mold their children up until puberty, despite some inadequacies. Not until separation from them has been accomplished do "mentors" in society at large tend to play a greater role. If one reads Levinson (1978) closely, it becomes clear that for him, being a mentor more or less means being a man. After mid-life, one should no longer look for mentors but be one. But what should a woman do, what meaning and substance can she give to her life when she can be no one's mentor and her children no longer need her?

An example should help to illustrate the extent to which a person's surmounting the problems of mid-life is dependent on existing emotional ties being broken or at least changed, and on the ability to set oneself new goals and tasks.

Judy married relatively late. For years she had lived with a man who had more or less forced her into the dominant role, leaving all responsibility for their shared life to her. Her feelings toward him were ambivalent. Finally she separated from him, though this caused her severe guilt. Shortly thereafter she married another man. She had worked before her marriage and continued to do so, interrupting her work only briefly when she gave birth to a child. Judy loved her daughter more than anything and later always reproached herself for not having sufficiently devoted herself to her. When Judy was forty-seven, her fifteen-year-old daughter began to separate herself from her, as was normal for that age. Judy grieved intensely that she had not done more at the time when the child was dependent on her and wondered if she might perhaps have neglected some things in her upbringing. Judy was fully aware, however, that her daughter was more easily able to separate herself from her—an independent mother who was satisfied with her career—than the children of some of her friends, whose mothers saw their children's dependence on them as the meaning of their lives. Even so, she continued to feel oppressed by a feeling of "lost happiness" and clung to the idea that she had not done enough for her daughter.

Thus the inevitable separation process, and her confrontation with growing older, were painful experiences for Judy. Her good relationship with her husband helped her to get over many things; with his help she learned to reduce her guilt (about having supposedly neglected her daughter) to a manageable level and overcame it to the extent that it no longer needlessly encumbered her relationship with her daughter.

Several years later, Judy had to come to terms with several more separation processes. She had to make do more and more without a sense of partnership in her relationship with her husband, who was increasingly weakened by a severe chronic illness. As she had during the time when her daughter was still small, she felt torn between the obligations of her career, her need for self-realization, and the wish to devote herself wholly to caring for someone else (in this case, her sick husband). Once again intense guilt feelings appeared; sometimes she discharged them by depressive reactions and sometimes by showing impatience toward her husband.

If we look at Judy's childhood, we find that she was very attached to her mother and suffered even as a small child from the fact that her mother was often unhappy in her marriage. The father (like her husband later) was ill for a long period of time; he was given to depression, demanded a great deal of attention from his wife, but himself possessed little empathy for his wife and daughter. Thus even as a child Judy had the feeling that she had to furnish her mother with what her father did not. But Judy was also aware that her mother clung to her too much and did not try hard enough to make herself independent and find meaning in her life outside of the family. This was also the reason that Judy herself took pains to continue working when she gave birth to a child; she was determined not to become wholly dependent on her family and their affection. It had taken her a long time to achieve what the psychoanalyst Margaret Mahler (1965) called separation-individuation. Her father had been incapable of providing her with the necessary "third person," whom the child needs in order to achieve release from the dyadic relationship with the mother. For the child, the relationship with the father represents a "door to the world" that offers the possibility of slowly becoming more independent and discovering that there are other fellow human objects in addition to the mother.

With Judy there had not been sufficient "triangulation," with this second relationship finally acquiring a meaning of its own, thus expanding the child's view of the world and her independence. Judy's father, or her image of him, could not relieve her of the responsibility that she felt for her mother. Although Judy later largely succeeded in achieving separation from her mother during puberty, with the help of extrafamilial interests, she was unable to escape these guilt feelings pertaining to her mother, which were disproportionate to reality. She continued to think of herself as the person who had to provide her mother with a substitute for unfulfilled hopes of happiness in marriage. At the same time, she needed to feel independent and had an irrepressible need to live her own life. These constellations repeated themselves, if in varied form, in her relationship with her daughter and later with her sick husband. She was often quite saddened at her inability to fulfill both of these equally strong needs; internally she believed she had to.

If Judy had largely succeeded in freeing herself from her great dependence on her mother during puberty, it was because her mother had helped her to do so much more than she had been able to perceive for a long time. The fact that it had taken her so long to be able to free herself from the harassing feeling of having to make her mother happy also had to do with her own attitudes and needs. For with the aid of this internal constellation, she had succeeded in preserving intact the feeling of being "the most important thing on earth" for another person.

The psychoanalyst Helene Deutsch portrayed a similar situation in her autobiography (1973). For her, the sorrows of old age begin when a person no longer feels this singular importance to anyone. Incidentally, one finds other problems in Helene Deutsch's life history that are amazingly similar to Judy's. Deutsch too complained of having neglected her son because she pursued her professional ambitions too resolutely. Her guilt and the feeling of having denied herself something of paramount importance in life accompanied her to the very end of her life. Her husband, who was sick over a long period of time, died while she was on a trip to Greece on which he had encouraged her to go. She could never forgive herself for this "hunger for the world," as she put it, after her husband died suddenly during her absence.

Often guilt feelings of this kind can be traced back only partly to close symbiotic bonding with the mother. In believing that one is "the most important thing on earth" to her, one has reversed the original mother-child relationship, making another person as dependent on oneself as that self was on its relationship to the mother at an earlier time.

Judy thus was not able to mourn and work through this early symbiotic relationship until mid-life; slowly, she learned to accept her daughter's need for separation and reduced her own guilt with respect to her daughter to a more appropriate level. With her husband's illness, she once again experienced the conflict between career, her own life, and the internal compunction to be a good, indispensable mother to others. This is not to say that there is anything wrong with the desire to help other people or to want to make them happy; it is simply that in this regard one must make one's own unconscious and exaggerated bonding needs conscious. Guilt feelings that accompany the desire for a life of one's own and for independence are an expression of serious conflicts between two contradictory needs; such guilt feelings often lead to depression and are of no help to anyone.

Only by learning to see through the past and one's past

behavior, and by accomplishing the work of mourning in order to slowly be able to separate from the past can something resembling a "new beginning" take place. With such internal separations and the new self-awareness that comes with them, the ambivalent relations between mother and daughter that are spoken of so often nowadays could also be improved. The mother is often made out to be the cause of whatever emotional problems her children, particularly her daughters, develop. The accusation that a mother does not release her daughters from dependency on her as they grown older is a hurtful one to a woman at mid-life, for she is already wondering how she will cope with loneliness when her children begin to separate from her. The husband, who is often entirely absorbed in his professional interests, rarely summons up sympathy or empathy for the loneliness of women at this time in life.

Little attention has been devoted to the fact that childhood dependence, which can continue into adult life, can also be shaped by a father who has not adequately taken part in the early-childhood upbringing of his daughter. The child needs this "third party," however, who must be not an enemy but rather a friend, indeed occasionally an extension of the mother, so that in its helplessness the child can free itself from a mother who is experienced as all-powerful and devote itself to its needs for independence more or less without fear.

9

Psychoanalysis and Emancipation

THE EMANCIPATION of women has become a fashionable topic in a cliché- and prejudice-ridden emotional debate between advocates and opponents. Everyone can count on the applause of their own faction by merely including the proper signals, inflammatory words, and slogans in their polemics. That the struggle for women's liberation has sometimes been grossly distorted ought to be an occasion for serious concern. In many areas of the world the status of women continues to be not only reprehensible, as in ours, but even a clear affront to human dignity. We may expect little change from gestures such as the "United Nations Year of the Woman," since institutions tend to become self-serving.

In conservative Germany, people are increasingly coming to think that the whole topic of emancipation has been discussed and rediscussed to death. Antifeminist books displaying meager knowledge or truth can become best-sellers—I would cite as an example Esther Vilar's *The Manipulated Man* ([1971] 1972). The *New York Review*

of Books has said of such books that they draw a picture
of women that is strongly reminiscent of anti-Semitic articles of the Nazi era. Just as the Jew was denounced as
a deceitful businessman and conscienceless exploiter, so
certain reactions of women toward habitual injustice are
branded as "typically female" in a grotesque distortion.
Neither the anti-Semite nor the antifeminist give any thought
at all to the historical and social circumstances that permit
only certain occupations to an oppressed portion of the
population or that force modes of behavior upon them
that are then used to legitimize domination, oppression,
and contempt.

The current wave of conservative, even reactionary,
nostalgia in West Germany would seem to take us back
not only to the 1920s and 1930s, but even further. A German government minister not long ago compared his work
with the "qualities" of a middle-class housewife: the less
that is heard from her, the better. Official sources thus
emphasized that a woman's good reputation is guaranteed
only when she behaves as quietly—that is as unpoliti-
cally—as possible and acquiesces passively and obediently
to social oppression.

In the past, career women could expect that such a
publicly expressed return to the mendacious double standard of the turn of the century would trigger widespread
indignation; they learned differently. But since women
continue to represent the majority of eligible voters, who
after all elected the present government, one cannot avoid
the impression that women have once again elected the
party that strives most fervently to thwart their attempts
at liberation.

Of course it must be admitted that women have hardly

been able to hold their own politically even in the so-called progressive parties and socialist countries. In an extensive study of 7,000 female workers in the countries of the European Economic Community, Helge Pross (1979) showed that in Western countries, women are as much as ever the victims of limited opportunities for promotion, low wages, the double burden of home and career, and so on. But the prevailing reaction to all of this is one of indifference. Women are certainly not furthering their chances for success by identifying with society's patronizing attitude toward their own sex.

But to return to the statement by the aforementioned government minister: Today's young people have become accustomed to an equivalence between the sexes, at least nominally. But for a public figure to make the qualities of the middle-class housewife into a measure of his own worth is a novelty. It challenges us not only to reflect on the current political situation of women but brings us to our actual subject, the relationship between psychoanalysis and the emancipation of women.

That the psychoanalytic concept of penis envy has been vehemently attacked by feminists is well-known. Freud's theory is seen as the incarnation of a male prejudice that contributes to maintaining the patriarchal order of society. Many feminists have reprimanded psychoanalysis in general for being reactionary and counterrevolutionary with respect to women's efforts toward liberation. Women are said to be jealous not of men's penises but of their greater social and professional freedom. It is clear that the conscious and unconscious consequences of centuries of social accretions are involved here.

What is the significance of the government minister's

position cited above? Why does he compare himself with a woman at all, let alone a woman from the turn of the century? Could this woman represent his own mother? Has he perhaps even made an identification with his mother, that is, a female identification? If that were so—and naturally this is only a hypothesis, to dissect someone on the couch in absentia is not my intention—then this would in no way be a rare psychological phenomenon.

Psychoanalysts speak not only of unconscious penis envy in women but of envy of childbearing in men. We are confronted ever more frequently with the fact that not only do women sometimes wish they were men, but that a man may harbor an unconscious wish to be a desirable woman. This wish awakens envy in him of women who can be what he cannot. Men who have grown up without fathers, as was almost the rule in Germany during both world wars, have been found to identify with women during the first years of childhood and afterward with particular frequency. It is well-known that a person who is jealous does not grant the envied person respect or acknowledge his or her successes. Often the opinions and modes of behavior born of unconscious envy are rationalized, for example, with the help of prejudices about the physical and mental inferiority of women. The young people in the leftist student subculture of the late 1960s were no exception in this respect. They preserved the same tendencies to scorn and denigrate women as all other layers of society. Considering that liberation from antifeminist prejudices and the struggle against the oppression of women were among their acknowledged political beliefs, this is astounding. The following is an example:

A student, Peter, sought psychoanalytic treatment for anxiety and depression. He was a member of a leftist alliance and lived in a communal household with several men and women. He wholeheartedly supported his female comrades who strove for an improvement in the political and social status of women. Like them, he was deeply enraged when confronted with social injustice and disregard for women.

His own relationships with women were quite complicated, however. He was incapable of becoming attached to a woman, no matter how lovable she might seem at first. Whenever he broke up with a woman he had succeeded in strongly binding to him, he showed no regard for the cruelty of his behavior. Upon closer examination it could be seen that wishes to denigrate women surfaced in his amorous relationships. He was defenseless against his feelings of envy. He was aware of an underlying need (though he could not explain it) to avenge himself on his girlfriends, and felt it as a triumph whenever he could break up with them just at the moment when their bond to him was especially strong.

In the course of the analysis it emerged that he behaved in a jealous and vengeful manner because his unconscious desire to be a desirable woman could not be fulfilled. An escape into homosexuality was not a possibility for him—perhaps because he had not succeeded in winning his father's love, in being loved by him like a girl.

Such unconscious wishes, and the feelings of envy and vengefulness that come with them, can also result in impotence in men. I am reminded of a patient who first met his father when he was seven years old. The patient, who was very much tied to his mother, married relatively late an attractive woman several years his senior. He was incapable of performing sexual intercourse in his marriage but masturbated daily. The analysis revealed that he begrudged his wife the gratification that he wished for himself. In his fantasy he remained the beloved daughter of a mother he had experienced as omnipotent and phallic. This bonding to his mother represented basically a negative Oedipus complex. The mother was the man, he the girl. The power that he imputed to his mother, and later to his wife—those women on whom he felt completely dependent while envying them for their attractiveness—had kindled a reactive need in him to degrade these women by sexually neglecting them.

Such constellations of contradictory emotional attitudes are found quite frequently; on the one hand, a man despises women, regarding them as by nature morally and mentally inferior, while on the other hand, he identifies with them and their position in society and fights for their liberation from sexual oppression and double standards. The Austrian satirist Karl Kraus was a typical example of this conflict. Although Freud certainly shared this male prejudice about the nature and destiny of women, he contributed as had no one before him to their liberation from the hypocritical sexual mores of his time. With the help of his method it was possible for the first time to systematically illuminate the motives behind such egoistic male idealization and simultaneous infantilization and degradation of women. In breaking the prohibition against thinking about sexual matters to which women in his society and time were subject, he took one of the most important steps, making it possible to change qualities that had been regarded as typically female and recognize them as culturally determined.

The demands of contemporary feminists are in many respects different from those of their predecessors at the beginning of the century. There are still calls for equal opportunity in education and on the job, equal pay for men and women, day-care centers for working mothers, and so on. But such demands now seem old-fashioned compared to today's battle cries and calls for a "Women's Revolution." Such women are fighting to make a basic change in the system, a change oriented toward specifically female needs, feelings, and modes of thought. They demand liberation from the obligation to bear children and much more. Often feminists retreat into lesbian relationships, considering men incapable of understanding the psyches of women. "At present there can be no healthy relationship between a man and a woman; perhaps in twenty years, but not now," said Margaret Sloane, a black spokesperson for radical feminists in the United States. Of course not all feminists are striving for a feminist revolution based on lesbian premises—but among intellectuals recent times have seen such prominent advocates as Simone de Beauvoir. Such women hold that only a lesbian relationship develops the full experiential capacity of a woman and contributes to her liberation from male domination.

Many feminists question the validity of marriage as an institution; it is said to merely suit men's needs to subjugate and own women. The history of marriage would seem to confirm this judgment. For millennia the institution of marriage rested on the ownership rights of men and on domination of women by a patriarchally ruled family. The Sixth Commandment—"What God hath joined, let no man put asunder"—was a reworking of the convention of a familial organization derived from economic and patriarchal-political interests, in accordance with a claim to dominance (Alexander Mitscherlich and Margarete Mitscherlich 1975). One portion of humanity lived enslaved to the other. Women were male property or exchangeable goods. In committing adultery, a woman was guilty of embezzling male property; the crime is still punished with incomparable brutality in some parts of the world.

Times have changed, and marriages of inclination have become the norm in our society, even if only relatively recently from a historical perspective. And just at this point in time, when a new relationship between the sexes might even become possible in marriage, that institution is coming under an attack the likes of which has never been seen before. When women become conscious of their denigration and psychological crippling, it would seem that their rage cannot easily be suppressed. The still-maintained assumption of male superiority, accepted without question by both sexes for centuries, makes a collision with male prejudices ever more unavoidable.

Certainly, psychological crippling imprinted over a period of centuries cannot be done away with easily, if at all. To my knowledge, the women's rights crusaders at the beginning of this century did not concern themselves at all with psychoanalysis and its appeal for greater sexual freedom for women. They fought for women's autonomy as individuals but were themselves little interested in sexual matters. Nor did they show any interest in the deterministic power that the unconscious exercises on human behavior. Psychoanalysis was evidently too revolutionary for them. Their identification with their society's prejudices prevented any serious interest in this science.

A great deal has changed, but the rejection of psycho-analysis by feminists has become even more fierce. Many regard Freud as Public Number Enemy One. Of the many factors that have contributed to maintaining a male-oriented society, they place the greatest blame on the Freudian concept of the psychosexual development of women (Figes 1974). To what extent is this criticism justified? The more thoughtful of these critics should be taken seriously. For it is not only feminists who have attacked Freud's theories about women; psychoanalysts themselves have always found the topic controversial.

"The great question that has never been answered, and which I have not been able to answer despite my thirty years of research into the female soul is: What do women want?" This statement by Freud in a conversation with the psychoanalyst Marie Bonaparte reflects a bewilderment that seems incomprehensible, considering that at the time Freud had already expounded his ideas about female development.

But what did Freud mean by his question? Was he—as a patriarchal father in accordance with the prevailing notions of his time—really unable to understand that a woman could want something in addition to a husband and a child (that is a supposed substitute for her own physical inferiority)? This hardly seems probable, for although he often spoke disparagingly about women in his writings and letters—they were narcissistic, incapable of cultivation and true object love, their dependence on men's opinions even went so far as to drive them to adopt men's disparagement of the female sex—Freud's thinking was on the other hand stamped by such an incorruptible search for the truth that he certainly would not have been satisfied with such clichés.

Certainly he underestimated the effect of sociocultural prejudices and constraints on the familial atmosphere and on child rearing.

From accounts of the famous Wednesday-evening discussions that Freud held for many years with his colleagues, pupils, and friends, it is clear that he regarded the social position of women as unchangeable. Motherhood prohibited the average woman from having a career. The struggle of feminists for a better status for women could thus benefit only a few select women, if any at all. Freud apparently had no sense of the changing situation of women. Thus he failed to recognize that his hypothesis of female penis envy rested in part on real familial and social disadvantages, but ones that might well be changed. Thus penis envy does not result *exclusively* from the childhood perception of the anatomical difference between the sexes, and Freud's ideas about female development remain one-sided.

> I cannot evade the notion (though I hesitate to give it expression) that for women the level of what is ethically normal is different from what it is in men. Their super-ego is never so inexorable, so impersonal, so independent of its emotional origins as we require it to be in men. Character-traits which critics of every epoch have brought up against women—that they show less sense of justice than men, that they are less ready to submit to the great exigencies of life, that they are more often influenced in their judgements by feelings of affection or hostility—all these would be amply accounted for by the modification of their super-ego which we have inferred above. We must not allow ourselves to be deflected from such conclusions by the denials of the feminists, who are anxious to force

us to regard the two sexes as completely equal in position and worth. (Freud [1925] 1963)

Freud's remarks were clearly conditioned by the time in which he lived. In the meantime, feminists are fighting for more than professional and economic equality; some have continued to confuse the struggle for equal rights with an irrational struggle for uniformity between the sexes. The most prominent feminists have long since stopped fighting for equality, however. For many, the last two world wars have shown that a world ruled by men will of necessity lead to the final destruction of all life. The "feminist revolution" is fighting today to give women greater influence and power over the formation of attitudes in society and political decisions. Women have more critical and more object-related attitudes toward the values of the past. They need this power in order to temper the destructive tendencies of male society and to be able to change circumstances that are bound to produce hatred. This dispute over humanity's self-alienation is the focal point of women's struggle.

For all of Freud's one-sidedness and occasionally unmistakable prejudices, we should not underestimate the brilliant and subtle capacity of his judgment. He researched women's complex psychic constellation as no one else has done and was sensitive to how it had come about through centuries of oppression.

But do Freud's ideas about female sexuality represent a comprehensive in-depth psychological picture of women's internal situation? In what other places are his theories questionable? Where do they purport to be apodictic when they are in fact limited by temporally bound prejudices? In order to offer a basis for evaluating Freud's theories about women, I would like to summarize the more controversial aspects and then discuss other psychoanalysts' ideas that dissent from them.

According to Freud, girls experience themselves as boys during the first years of childhood, which are so decisive for later development. Not until a girl perceives the anatomical difference between the sexes is she forced to recognize what Freud characterizes as "reality." The perception of being disadvantaged by nature is supposedly the reason that a girl finally decides to be female. A woman who refuses to compensate by developing wishes proper to her sex, who clings in her fantasy to her own completeness, and is unwilling to give up clitoral sensations characterized as "phallic," does not (according to Freud) achieve mature femininity, which is expressed not only in the wish to have children but also in the ability to attain vaginal orgasm.

In other words, Freud assumed that women's psychic processing of the anatomical difference between the sexes leaves them with no choice but to experience themselves as fundamentally impaired. He considered it a sign of maturity for a woman to succeed during the course of puberty in completely suppressing the sexual excitations emanating from the clitoris.

Such theories of immature clitoridal and mature vaginal sexuality have in my opinion actually contributed to intensifying women's feelings of inferiority and increasing their envy of men. For under such circumstances, women must envy men not only for their privileged position in society but for being able to yield to their genital needs without this provoking feelings of inferiority, and for suffering less frequently from difficulty in attaining orgasm. In our times, bent as they are on high productivity—even in sexual matters—this inadequacy is especially damaging to a person's self-esteem.

In psychoanalysis, we proceed from the phase-related libidinal zones, using them to represent the various stages of psychological development and the object relations and needs associated with them. For a person to cling to certain forms of gratification is understood as fixation or regression. We tend to assume that the causes of such behavior are to be found in childhood conflicts: misunderstandings between parent and child, spoiling or depriving the child, and so forth.

Just as in childhood sexual forms of gratification of an anal or oral nature are repressed with disgust at a more developed stage, let us say an Oedipal one, so during puberty a young girl turns against her clitoridal sexuality, which represents a vestige of her male-phallic phase (according to Freud in a letter to Fliess dated November 14, 1897). Upon rereading this text, one is at a loss to understand how a thinker as critical as Freud could fail to recognize a pubescent girl's shame and repression of sexual impulses as the consequence of social demands and morals and could continue to regard this as a psycho-biological process of maturation. How could Freud believe that with puberty, then, there is an increase in the libido of boys but a fresh wave of repression of sexuality in girls? That such ideas are completely unbiological renders them even more astounding. Freud's analytical and medical observations could easily have taught him that the sexual upsurge that takes place during puberty is as strong in girls as in boys.

In his *Three Essays on the Theory of Sexuality,* Freud explained sexual repression in women during puberty, which he regarded as natural, as follows: "The intensification of the brake upon sexuality brought about by pubertal repression in women serves as a stimulus to the libido in men and causes an increase of its activity. Along with this heightening of libido there is also an increase of sexual overvaluation which only emerges in full force in relation to a woman who holds herself back and who denies her sexuality" ([1905] 1963). Considering that Freud was quite clear about the detrimental influence a society's attitude toward sexuality and its mendacious double standard could have on women's development, it is all the more incongruous that he was also of the opinion that inhibited sexuality in a woman was the precondition for a man's being able to develop a full sexual and emotional desire for her. In the meantime we have a more than ample supply of evidence that no such laws prevail between the sexes, and that at the very least sexual excitability in men does not depend on the negative attitude of women. Experiments with rhesus monkeys conducted by the English researcher Dr. Michael showed that sexual activity of the male animals is dependent on the favorable hormonal status of the females (Gillespie 1975). Human relationships are of course more complex and more easily disrupted, but we do know that over the course of long-lasting sexual relationships, the potency of the man is frequently dependent on the sexual desires of the woman. Only in a social order in which rule by "strong" men is taken for granted could ideas about the conquest and forcible subjugation of women be experienced as particularly exciting sexually and leave a corresponding imprint on the fantasies of women as well.

More recent research has demonstrated unequivocally that the embryological theory that the clitoris is a stunted male organ is wrong. The so-called inductor theory of primary sexual differentiation has been strengthened by the study of embryos. In the course of these studies it was found that during the first weeks of life the embryo is neither undifferentiated nor androgenous but anatomically female (Sherfey [1966] 1972).* In order to masculinize the originally female organs of reproduction, the genetically male embryo requires the hormone androgen. In contrast, the development of female characteristics represents an autonomous maturation of an inborn predisposition. Both sexes thus appear to be phenotypically female during their initial embryonic stages of development; thus the clitoris is a part of the female genitalia from the very beginning.

In order to avoid misunderstandings, it should be said that psychoanalysts do not overestimate the role of biology in psychosexual development; it is simply that it must be clearly defined so that some of Freud's theoretical notions that were derived from contemporary biological notions can be recognized as erroneous. Since the clitoris is not a stunted male organ—and, in fact, it may be assumed that the phallus is an enlarged clitoris—there is no biological basis for a phallic phase in a girl. Naturally this does not mean that the existence and symbolic meaning of the phallus does not provoke characteristic reactions in a little girl. The role played by the psychic processing of the anatomical difference between the sexes and its symbolism has

---

* The researcher K. L. Moor arrived at different conclusions; according to Moor, the mammal embryos he studied are undifferentiated in the beginning, neither male nor female. See Eissler 1977.

been described by many authors, although interpreted differently.

Nor can it be regarded as a sign of biological or psychic maturity if in the course of her development a woman abandons clitoral stimulation in favor of vaginal. The clitoris's capacity for stimulation is a full physiological part of sexual gratification in women. As everyone must know by now, the purely vaginal orgasm is a myth. This however does not mean, as is often erroneously claimed, that there is no such thing as a vaginal orgasm—many women experience them—it is just that physiologically the clitoris, as well as certain muscle contractions, blood vessels, nerves, and so on participate in producing an orgasm. The psychic significance of the sexual act and the type of orgasm should not be underestimated, however. It makes a difference whether the sexual act alleviates or aggravates anxieties with respect to the intactness of one's own body, whether the good symbiotic relationship to the mother is repeated, whether guilt feelings are assuaged or reactivated—there is no denying that pleasurable feelings associated with the genital act depend not only on physiological factors but to a great degree on psychological ones.

A child's perception of the genital difference between the sexes is now thought by many researchers to occur at a much earlier age than Freud believed—namely before the phallic phase of development. It is assumed that this difference is generally perceived by the end of the second year of life at the latest. In addition, a number of observers of child behavior have determined that the behavior of boys and girls begins to differ even before the phallic phase. It is doubtful, however, that such gender-specific behavior is a consequence of a child's psychic processing of the recognition of the anatomical difference. Hence, for example, the research of Stoller (1968, 1974), which concluded that girls and boys develop according to the way they are raised—that is, according to how their gender is defined after birth, even if this does not correspond to their biological gender.

The sources of sexual identity have been much discussed in the wake of more recent studies of transsexuals, transvestites, and homosexuals, and many previous views have been called into question. According to these researchers, sexual identity is determined by children on the basis of the way they are brought up and the way their environment behaves toward them. Thus sexuality does not depend on a child's biological gender or on external sexual characteristics. This self-determination of gender on the part of the child is said to develop during the first year of life. The so-called core gender of the child—that is, the child's feeling of being male or female—apparently develops in accordance with the gender to which the child is assigned at birth. Self-determination of gender is believed by several researchers to be completed at the age of eighteen months, and by others as late as the third year of life. After this point, the process is more or less irreversible, and psychic developmental problems may be expected if attempts are made to take a child with a false gender determination and reraise that child in accordance with its biological gender.

Sexual self-classification is believed to be closely related to the child's capacity for psychic organization, identity, and self-representation. For choices of object and of identity are bound up with gender identity, as Stoller (1975) and others have argued. That is, people seek out other human objects for imitation and identification in accordance with their own gender identity (see also Person 1974).

That the symptoms of transsexuality and transvestitism are found more frequently in men than in women is considered an indication of the great difficulties a boy has in identifying himself as consistently male. The first object of identification for both sexes is the mother; it is above all a boy who must effect the readjustment to another object. This contradicts some of the research of Stoller (1975) and Person (1974), however, who found that boys and girls develop in accordance with their diagnosed gender as early as shortly following birth. This would mean that from the very beginning, multiple possibilities for identification are present, or that various forms of identification with the mother occur. It is one thing for a boy or a girl to identify with the mother's body and her gender-related capabilities such as nursing, menstruating, giving birth, and so on; it is another to identify with modes of behavior that are in no way necessarily gender-specific and are only regarded as such by a given society. Qualities such as empathy and capacity for love do not have to conflict with a child's "core gender." If "core gender identity" is indeed formed within the context of the parent-child relationship, it is above all the parents' *attitudes* toward certain qualities and types of behavior that cause the child to regard them as male or female.

Many people develop occasional confusion about their gender identity without fundamentally calling it into question, as for instance do transsexuals and some homosexuals and transvestites. That means that as early as the first years of life, a multiplicity of human relations and the possibility for internalization exists—a multiplicity that need not be based on gender identity and will lead to confusion only if the parents or society impose gender-specific restrictions.

René Spitz's observations about a child's early idealization of the mother and the ensuing socialization suggest an assumption of a primary femininity that develops through identification. Only in the course of further development and as a result of an ever-growing capacity to apprehend reality—whether it be the reality of the anatomical difference between the sexes or of the differing social appraisals of the two sexes—can a child reach the point where it (i.e., the child) can no longer overlook that there are two differently valued sexes, and work through this fact accordingly.

Freud's theories arose from the interpretations he gave to his patients' recollections, fantasies, dreams, neurotic symptoms, and behavior. He began with frequently perplexing psychological observations and attempted to understand them by classifying them according to type and relating them to various biological stages of maturation. For him, a girl's turn toward her father was not the expression of natural female needs but the result of complex, conflict-producing psychic reworkings of certain perceptions and conflict-associated experiences with the mother.

Freud's psychoanalysis was concerned with the *psychic* working-through of conflict-producing psychobiological processes of maturation. This has been forgotten by the psychoanalytical revisionists such as Horney, Sullivan, and others when they reproach Freud for being "biological." But they themselves, for example Horney, speak of "natural femininity," "natural sexual power of attraction," and so forth; they thus think in more narrowly biological categories than did Freud himself. For Freud nothing was natural—that is, nothing in human beings is by nature simple and free from conflict. That he saw and interpreted some things differently than we would today should not surprise us.

To see the alleged displacement of the site of sexual stimulation from the clitoris to the vagina as a sign of psychosexual maturation was an error, for example; this error was based not only on contemporaneous false notions about physiology, biology, and embryonic development but on the idea of the predominance of men in society, one that demanded passivity from women as a counterpart. If the sexual needs of women were no different from those of men, and if women could satisfy those needs not just passively or in a masochistic pleasure at being subjugated, then the preconceived notions of male predominance would be undermined.

Freud's theory about the genesis and development of penis envy is not shared by all psychoanalysts. The views of Karen Horney (1967) differed from those of Freud. In her opinion, primary penis envy develops on the one hand out of a narcissistic overestimation of the process of excretion during the anal phase, and on the other through infantile pleasure in looking at others and exhibiting oneself, in which the boy is at an advantage; finally, primary penis envy develops because boys are permitted, in fact taught, to grasp their penises when they urinate, something a small girl interprets as permission to masturbate. Horney did not believe that the discovery of the anatomical difference between the sexes could itself explain penis envy. In addition, she held the concept of penis envy to be superfluous in explaining a small girl's turn from the mother toward the father. This switch, she asserted, simply expresses an elementary natural process, namely the attraction of each sex for the other. Freud's comment: "A solution of ideal simplicity," which unfortunately did not accord with the results of laborious psychoanalytic investigations.

On the basis of my own clinical experience, I have arrived at the conclusion that the phase in a little girl that corresponds to the phallic phase in a little boy needs to be defined as clitoral in order to make clear that the clitoris is an independent organ and not a stunted penis and does not need to be experienced primarily as such. When we observe a phallic phase in a girl, as is the case, I would agree with Jones (1933, 1935) and Horney that frequently we are dealing here with a defense against the Oedipus complex, which has awakened anxiety and led to identification with the father. In the process, a girl's comparison of herself with her father can call forth envy, but an identification with the father can also release feelings of worthlessness if the father is not respected by the mother or the social environment.

That the phallic phase in a little boy is a defensive one from the start, as Jones (1933) asserts, does not seem accurate to me. Certainly concentration on the phallus and its significance, as well as fear of losing it, can later lead to phallic narcissism that is surely defensive in nature and is expressed particularly when a strong unconscious wish to be female must be warded off. But the maturation from oral and anal to phallic or clitoridal-vaginal phenomena represents a development of the libido that in my opinion can be observed in all children. As recent research has demonstrated, during childhood, the pituitary gland produces the greatest amount of hormones between the fourth and sixth years of life; the genital organs do not react with visible changes, however, as happens during puberty. Only somatic sensations, that is stimulations of a phallic or clitoral nature, increase at this time. With each successive stage of biological and psychosexual maturation, the wishes associated with primary objects also change.

The phallic phase in a boy is tied up with Oedipal wishes for his mother, the clitoral phase in a girl with wishes for the love of her father. Here, at least according to the experience and observations of most analysts, it is not merely a question of an uncomplicated attraction between the sexes but of the complex result of a gender-specific, pre-Oedipal relationship to the mother.

I would also concur with Jones and Horney that a girl's phallic phase—her desire to be a man as an expression of her secondary penis envy—represents the result of defensive operations, whereas the clitoral or clitoral-vaginal developmental stage, with its disappointments with the mother and its positive Oedipal desires, should be regarded as a phase of object relations appropriate to girls, one that goes hand in hand with a peak in childhood genital somatic sensations. I am describing these processes in such detail in order to make clear how difficult it is to understand the complex process of female development. The unconscious repressed consequences on the adult woman of childhood experiences is overlooked or passed over by many feminists as insignificant.

Experiences with adult female patients and interpretations of their fantasies, recollections, and behavior suggest that a small girl does not experience herself primarily as a little man, despite her intense wish to possess the mother for herself alone. On the other hand, one cannot explain her turn toward her father solely on the basis of innate femininity and the attraction between the sexes. Disappointment with the father contributes to a little girl's casting about during the Oedipal stage for a new object, one from whom she hopes for greater satisfaction. It is only in the course of her development, and on the basis of the twin fear of loss of love and the destruction of the interior of the body, that a little girl abandons her genital wishes with regard to her father.

Whether the original disappointment with the mother can indeed be traced back to the fact that the mother is seen as the person who withholds the penis from the girl, as Freud believed, is a question that cannot be answered unequivocally. Many other disappointments and deidealizations or actual experiences of being denigrated must be added to the experience of the inferiority of being female in order to lead to a turn away from the mother toward the father. Chasseguet-Smirgel seems to be right in many cases: With a girl's increasing knowledge of reality, the possession of a penis is unconsciously regarded as offering the possibility of opposing the omnipotent, envied mother with a narcissistic value of one's own.

It is doubtless important to recognize early-childhood factors in order to understand the behavior of an adult woman. However, the parent-child relationship cannot be envisioned as though it stood in no relation to the manifold influences of its environment. For it is just this combination of the consequences of childhood fantasies and experiences with the influence of group behavior, group ideals, and contemporaneous morality that lies at the root of a woman's behavior within her society.

The accusation that women are never free of ambivalence (just as a mother is always ambivalent with respect to her daughter), and that herein they are fundamentally different from men, seems to me to be only partly justified. Men can love as well as hate, it is said, because they are able to distribute love and hate better with respect to two persons: the mother is loved, the father hated. This too is only a partial truth. Neither sex is spared disappointments during the oral, anal, and phallic-clitoral stages, and later during the genital phase; in both, ambivalences, projections, and feelings of hatred persist with respect to the parents.

For the generation of Helene Deutsch and other early female psychoanalysts, the highest happiness was to find a husband and to be a part of a socially recognized marriage, and to bear children. For a long time people in the women's movement were ashamed to want to be mothers or to be maternal. Feminists saw in such needs a contemptible vestige of preemancipatory times. Today, even in parts of the women's movement, a reversal has taken place. Nostalgia and so-called new motherhood are the catchwords. "Self-realization" by living out motherhood to the fullest has been given a new lease on life.

Today one frequently has the impression that long after puberty both sexes are compelled to make up for childhood needs. Hardly anyone seems prepared to assume a maternal or paternal posture and to take on the burden of responsibility and care for others. Both men and women apparently long for the role of the desired and desirable woman, who as the mother's or father's darling is the center of attention. In the age of television, it should come as no surprise that narcissistic-exhibitionistic wishes are becoming more intense. But we psychoanalysts tend to see the deeper causes for this in the primary object relations, the relations to the parents during childhood.

Many young people today live in communal groups. In order to gain approval (without which they feel lost and rejected), they feel compelled to identify with the attitudes of the group. When parents cannot satisfy their children's needs for idealization, the children frequently find satisfaction for these needs in a group according to whose values they can orient their own. Although groups can serve the purpose of providing emancipatory stability for women and allowing working mothers to pursue their work in peace and can liberate them from the negative, egocentric, and constricting ties of the typical small family structure, they clearly cannot substitute for the intensity and continuity of successful family relationships and their structure-forming internalizations. Some groups have ideals but no superego that compels them from within to fulfill these ideals. For this they need external pressure. Frequently the need of group members for stimulation is so great that ideals must be changed repeatedly. In order to retain their power over group members, leaders of such groups often resort to manipulative measures. Moreover, sexual relationships in such groups would seem less to serve the purpose of satisfying genital needs than of satisfying early-childhood desires for idealization and love.

According to our observations, women who had been manipulated by such values found it especially important to overcome a scorned ideology of ownership. When they believed they were in a position to share everything with others, even their bodies and their most intimate thoughts, they had fulfilled their quasi-religious demands upon themselves. Their form of "self-realization" consisted in renouncing subjective middle-class needs, as they called them. They demanded of themselves that they no longer have any secrets from one another. The ability to be alone was neither cultivated nor regarded as a worthy goal. Thought impulses developing from within, concern with their own inner sensations, feelings, and values had little or no value at all for them. They remained almost wholly unaware that even so they had not been able to rid themselves of an ideal of sexual achievement that they consciously rejected—they were supposed to be "good" sexual performers, and they challenged one man after another to confirm that they were.

While in Freud's time a rigid sexual double standard had led women to repress their sexual needs, women are now under pressure to perform sexually, and in this way are no less sexually exploited than their mothers who live in monogamous marriages. They do not allow themselves to discover their own true needs; feelings such as jealousy, shame, a woman's wish to be alone with one partner and share her sexual experiences with him have all become new taboos, as illustrated by the following example:

Nora was the only child of middle-class parents. She had always perceived it as her responsibility to hold together her parents' shaky marriage. Both her father and mother worked. At first, Nora idealized her father, but then her mother became more successful, and became in Nora's opinion the truly active and guiding force in the family. Nora was very dependent on her mother up until she was nineteen years old. After completing high school, she attended an arts and crafts school.

She came in contact with artists who knew far more

about art and literature than she did and she was ashamed of her ignorance. When she asked to go back and get her secondary school diploma, her parents agreed and later supported her in beginning a course of study at the university as well. There she met students who were politically active, and she soon made herself entirely dependent on their ideals and views.

Nora lived in a commune and joined a group that belonged to the so-called hard core of politically active students. She entered into numerous sexual relationships with these students, whom she was able to admire and idealize, even if only for a short while. The deidealization that usually set in after a brief time on one side or the other was, however, not the only factor leading her to a quick change of lovers. Rather, it seemed that an unconscious need for punishment prevented her from having a satisfying sexual relationship. Apparently she had no right to fare better than her parents, whose rather unsatisfactory marriage had, after all, been kept together only for her sake. In her current relationships, Nora sometimes played the role of the desirable woman, allowing herself to be admired, and sometimes played the role of her father, feeling herself inferior. She either admired or was herself admired; ultimately all of these relationships came to an unhappy end. Nora suffered from guilt feelings that she repressed but then acted out in her unhappy friendships, because guilt feelings with respect to her parents or parent figures were taboo in her group.

The Oedipal conflict and the pre-Oedipal relationship to the mother vary from individual to individual; moreover, they are often determined by a given culture in accordance with the child-rearing practices of the particular social stratum. The so-called feminine traits are a

product of a given society's style of child rearing and predominant values; it is these values that determine what is
to be regarded as "femininity," female role behavior, maternal obligations, and so forth. For all of this, there are
many examples in history and ethnology. Parin, Morgenthaler, and Parin-Matthèy (1971), Margaret Mead (1928),
and other psychoanalysts and ethnologists have observed
that women in primitive cultures are able to fill the most
varied social roles. Most women in our culture have suffered the fate of all despised or degraded groups: For a
long time they possessed only a weakly developed feeling
of solidarity. This appears to be slowly changing. Women
are also reproached for uncritical conformity, lack of fighting spirit, and lack of determination in standing up for
their rights. Here too it is a matter of identifications and
types of behavior that over the course of millennia were
forced upon women as the weaker part of a male-dominated society. The precondition for liberation from such
behavioral constraints is the liberation of women from
social, economic, and familial oppression.

10

Narcissism and Masochism–
Typically Feminine?

PSYCHOANALYSIS HAS BEEN concerned from the very beginning with the unconscious processes that lie behind people's conscious motivations. With his metapsychology, Freud attempted to formulate a theory of the unconscious, a theory substantially different from forms of psychology that had prevailed up until that time.

In their clinical practice psychoanalysts soon recognized that they would achieve very little by the direct communication of the unconscious content and significance that lay behind their patients' words and actions or neurotic symptoms. Patients could not or would not understand what they were told when it was uncomfortable, insulting, anxiety-producing, or incomprehensible, and, moreover, called into question the opinions and appraisals that they had heretofore had of themselves.

Their "ego" defended itself against such interpretations with all its might. The patients had, after all, spent a lifetime building up a system of defense against perceptions and knowledge that might unleash considerable anxiety or mental suffering. All people have their own characteristic system of defense that fundamentally influences their ways of reacting.

Practicing psychoanalysts were thus forced to concern themselves more with the ego and its mechanisms of defense in order to help their patients to better understand themselves. Analysts learned in this way how best to approach their patients to make comprehensible to them what made them sick or their lives neurotically difficult. The psychology of the unconscious and of the id was expanded by the psychology of the ego and its—usually unconscious—mechanisms of defense.

In more recent times, psychoanalysts have found themselves confronted ever more frequently with the so-called narcissistic neuroses—that is with people whose feeling of self-esteem is undermined or whose capacity for relationships is stunted because their interest is centered almost exclusively on themselves and their own problems.

Many psychoanalysts today focus on the significance of the formation of a stable sense of self-esteem for human development. There is much discussion about whether the sickness of modern man and his feeling of meaninglessness and isolation are not to be found primarily in a disruption of his feeling of self and self-respect. In psychoanalysis one hears less of "where id was, there ego shall be" (which also implies a strong superego or conscience in the sense of traditional culture-bearing factors) than in Freud's time; instead, people prefer to talk of "authentic" or "basic personality," of "identity," and, above all, of the "self."

The American psychoanalyst Heinz Kohut has written several books investigating the complex development of a "true" or "false" self. Kohut ([1973] 1985) has pointed out the consequences that may ensue when a person is not capable of idealizing his or her parents in a phase-specific manner. When the ability to idealize the parents, internalize them, and thus use them as a secure basis for superego formation is repressed in childhood, the individuals so affected later suffer the consequences of a deficiency in superego and self-esteem. We then confront the inner insecurity of a narcissistically disoriented personality. To be sure, this insecurity is free from a so-called negative conscience, that is, from unconscious and conscious guilt feelings and the need for punishment; but in return the person is beset by feelings of shame, unreality, emptiness, and lack of goals.

But what do we mean by *narcissistic?* The concept goes back to the legend of Narcissus, who fell in love with his own reflection in the water. Thus narcissism is a love one directs not toward another person but toward an image of oneself; the concept is often used derogatorily. In so doing it is forgotten that only people who love and respect themselves are capable of loving others. A healthy narcissism, that is, the capacity to value oneself, is therefore to be distinguished from its pathological distortions, in which, for example, relations with other people are used exclusively to serve the purpose of self-aggrandizement or self-confirmation—or, at worst, play hardly any role at all.

The development of a stable feeling of self-esteem in a girl, however, remains in doubt due to our form of child rearing and the conscious and unconscious attitudes of the parents and society toward her. When women are characterized as narcissistic, the term is almost always intended derogatorily. Those who so argue hold women to be incapable of overcoming their excessive needs for admiration. Because of their egocentric attitudes, women are supposedly in no position to feel solidarity with members of their own sex.

According to Freud, too, women are more narcissistic than men because they are said to be unable to overcome the insult of lacking a penis, a symbol of power and completeness. Freud wrote: "We thus attribute a larger amount of narcissism to femininity, which also affects women's choice of object, so that to be loved is a stronger need for them than to love. The effect of penis envy has a share, further, in the physical vanity of women, since they are bound to value their charms more highly as a late compensation for their original sexual inferiority" ([1933] 1963). Freud's opinion is still shared by most psychoanalysts.

Although psychoanalysts are in agreement about the importance of establishing a stable feeling of self-esteem in the development of all human beings, in psychoanalytic circles one still hears disparaging talk of "typically" feminine narcissism. Women are held to be incapable of love because, as a result of their excessive need for admiration and being loved, they focus egocentrically on their own self-image. But just what constitutes women's narcissism and men's capacity to relate to others is not presented very convincingly in these arguments. Thus one may read in Béla Grunberger (1964a) that the "narcissistic" woman devotes herself to someone in order to be loved, whereas the (nonnarcissistic) man seeks gratification of a sexual drive, granting his partner narcissistic confirmation only in order to attain a drive-related goal. In other words, a woman who seeks love is narcissistic; a man for whom a woman represents merely a sexual object is not. Women's tendency to form lasting love relationships, rather than turning, like men, to "more serious matters" after falling in love for a brief while, continues to be characterized as typical feminine narcissism.

Psychoanalysis, in essence, gives two reasons for women's supposedly being at the mercy of their narcissistic needs: in the first place, the aforementioned insurmountable feeling of their own anatomical inferiority; in the second, the ambivalent love of a mother for her daughter. Grunberger (1964a) asserted that a small girl is never in a position to supply her own narcissistic confirmation because her mother withholds unqualified approval from her. The reason for this is said to lie in the nature of human drives: Mother and daughter cannot be adequate sexual objects for one another, and thus the love between them is supposedly never unequivocal and always ambivalent.

Both Grunberger and Freud regard unalterable givens—for one a biological-sexual given, for the other an anatomical given—as the source of women's deeply rooted feelings of inferiority and of the narcissistic orientation toward the self that develops from them. Only the birth of a son is considered to compensate for a woman's deficiency in self-esteem. The relationship between mother and son is thus seen as the most perfect human relationship. Freud wrote: "The difference in a mother's reaction to the birth of a son or a daughter shows that the old factor of lack of a penis has even now not lost its strength. A mother derives unlimited satisfaction from her relationship with a son; this is altogether the most perfect, the most free from ambivalence of all human relationships" ([1933] 1963). Here the mother acquired a value that Freud elsewhere denied her.

The meaning of the mother for the development of her

children, whether boys or girls, has in the meantime been researched thoroughly by numerous psychoanalysts. The development of a feeling of self-esteem in both son and daughter is dependent on the mother's empathy to her children's needs. Psychoanalytic theories about women are self-contradictory: On the one hand, a woman is held to be particularly narcissistic because she has been unable to develop a healthy feeling of self-esteem due to the aforementioned early-childhood injuries; on the other, it is regarded as normal that a mother can empathize with the small child as no other family member can. The view of "the mother as destiny" (Schottlander, 1946) still has validity for most psychoanalysts. Impossible demands are made on the mother. How is a woman supposed to provide what a mother is expected to in the way of love and empathy if she herself has never been granted love free from ambivalence, as psychoanalytic theories suggest? Disturbances of empathy in the mother-child relationship are rightly accorded enormous importance in the child's development, but the burden of guilt hereby placed on the mother is suffocating. Excessive demands are made on the mother, who is at the same time idealized.

No one has yet provided an explanation for why mothers are nevertheless frequently able to summon up surprising amounts of empathy, even though their own feelings of self-esteem were supposedly deeply disturbed at an early age. Presumably, internalizations of the anxiety-alleviating and consoling mother are passed on more permanently from generation to generation in girls than in boys, who are more or less forced by their society's norms of conduct to dissociate themselves from their first internalizations. Such early internalizations, which create the first psychic structures, often appear in girls to outlast later denigration of the mother (occurring as a defense against feelings of dependence and disappointment) and are apparently not extinguished by the social disparagement of women usually shared by the mother herself.

Perhaps a girl's early internalizations of maternal roles and the relationship to her mother contribute to the formation of a more structured self-image than is granted to boys, who are compelled in contrast to abandon their identification with the mother's roles by the external environment as well as the mother herself. The development of a memory for early experiences and feelings is often stunted in boys by this enforced rupture of identification. The evocative ability of memory to summon up objects before one's inner eye as needed—that is, to recall other human relationships and their consoling and anxiety-alleviating functions—may, for the aforementioned reasons, be more pronounced in girls than in boys, despite all later disturbances due to identification with self-devaluating maternal attitudes.

In some authors who plead for more narcissistic confirmation for both children and adults, one notes that far more attention is given to disturbances associated with the development of narcissism in men than to comparable disturbances in women.

Kohut (1973) regards it as proven that maternal admiration of the child is crucial to the development of a feeling of self-esteem and the integration of psychic structures into an independent self. The mother must show understanding of the child's need to show off, to elicit amazement and enthusiasm by its progress and achievements. It is supposedly of equally great psychic significance for the child to be given the opportunity to idealize an adult. For this it is above all the father who is responsible; he should thus adopt an appropriate role with respect to his child.

Kohut mentioned the problems of female development only briefly, arriving at the conclusion that little girls have similar needs to those of little boys. Occasionally a mother may also satisfy the little girl's need for idealization. In any case, a pathological development of the self may be reckoned with if there is a lack of models to be idealized.

The admiring mother and the admired father are supposed to be internalized during the course of development, so that the child can acquire feelings of self-esteem and inner security—feelings that are the foundation of a secure personality structure. The "gleam in the mother's eye"—that is her admiration for her child—is bestowed primarily upon boys, at any rate according to psychoanalytic theories. Just what is to become of a girl, who can expect only ambivalence from the mother (see Freud, Grunberger, and other analysts)? Kohut, too, fails to answer this question.

In Kohut's model (1973), male concepts of a patriarchal social order and its values are legitimized anew. According to this model, society can only serve the needs of children—thus fulfilling the conditions for the construction of a healthy feeling of self-esteem—when the father can be idealized and the mother can admire her child, that is of course, above all her son.

As analysts have stressed repeatedly, it is defenses against an early-childhood dependence on a mother who is experienced as omnipotent, as well as defences against envy of the ability to give birth, that must be regarded as the deeper sources of the widespread denigration of women. The persistence of the notion of a typically feminine narcissism probably also contributes to this denigration, behind which lurks a fear of one's own incapacity for love and defenses against the hatred that is born of excessive dependence and envy.

As a rule, it is rare for men to forego their need to be spoiled and admired by a maternal woman; thus they force women into a maternal and nurturing role in marriage as well. Men make women into mothers, and not the other way around, as Freud claimed when he wrote: "Even a marriage is not made secure until the wife has succeeded in making her husband her child as well and in acting as a mother to him" ([1933] 1963).

A girl's chances of developing a stable feeling of self-esteem still remain highly uncertain, owing to the conscious and unconscious attitudes of the parents. As soon as the girl's perception has developed sufficiently for her to recognize (consciously or unconsciously) the differing social estimations of the sexes, she frequently turns away from the denigrated and usually ambivalent mother and begins to idealize her father, attempting to win recognition from him. At the same time, the girl recognizes the often childishly dependent behavior of her father, who often experiences and treats his own children as rivals. On the one hand, the girl identifies with her father, who is more highly esteemed socially; on the other hand, she secretly despises him for his childish, egoistic dependence. But since the father is also a "self object"—that is, a part of the girl's own self—to her his merit or lack of merit also implies a judgment about herself. The already conflicting attitudes toward the mother are joined by a similarly ambivalent relationship to the father. Since she can admire him too only halfheartedly, her own feeling of self-esteem is diminished.

Intense defensive narcissism in a woman is occasionally the result of damage to her feeling of self-esteem as a child. She then endeavors above all to elicit the envy of her own sex as well as the admiration and regard of the other. In this way she may become a caricature of a woman, like those the male press has always portrayed with particular pleasure. She dresses provocatively; flirts with men constantly; is primarily interested in clothes, cosmetics, and shopping; and so forth. Even her relationships with her husband and children serve principally to compensate for her own lack of a feeling of self-esteem. Husband and child must at all costs be socially successful in areas in which she has not been able to be.

Are women more narcissistic than men? Or are they more capable of loving? In our culture perhaps both are true. A woman's sense of self is wounded too often for her not to need narcissistic compensation—that is, she has to contend more than a man does with feelings of inferiority and therefore is often at greater pains than he is to be loved and admired. In our culture, women are typically more able to put the interests of others before their own than men are; after all, they have been taught to do so from the start. Moreover, women are not as inclined to debase their sexual partners as sex objects.

Most women do not know why they often esteem themselves so little. They do not know that they are still identifying with male ideas about the "value" of a woman—ideas according to which a woman's function is to be beautiful, young, and successful, or maternal and self-sacrificing. Only when women divest themselves of such ideals of femininity will they be able to raise the standing of their own sex and in raising their children also represent it as worthy of emulation.

Many controversies have been ignited by the question of whether masochism is a typically female trait. In connection with male violence against women, particularly rape, one frequently hears the claim that women provoke such acts, that they even call forth violence from men through their masochistic desire for sexual submission. The humiliations and insinuations that usually lie in store for a woman who decides to press charges following a rape are all too well known. Thus in most cases rapes remain unreported and unatoned for. Frequently in legal proceedings, the more a woman is emotionally upset by degrading investigative methods, the more her credibility is called into question. Now, as in the past, most men cling to the opinion that women provoke rape by their behavior.

Even Freud, it is said, claimed that women typically develop fantasies in which they experience being raped as pleasurable. It is true that in psychoanalysis it has often been contended that women are by nature masochistic—that is, that they supposedly display a tendency to self-torment and pleasure in suffering. Freud believed that child rearing and the attitudes of society, as well as the psychic consequences of their biological/anatomical destiny, left women no other choice than to turn their aggression against themselves and in so doing to develop masochistic pleasure in suffering. Moreover, their masochism could supposedly be regarded as the precondition of their being able to enjoy sexual intercourse at all.

Masochism was originally understood in psychiatry as a perversion in which sexual gratification was linked with pain and humiliation. This notion was expanded in psychoanalytic theory. Freud distinguished between moral, erogenous, and feminine masochism. In moral masochism, unconscious guilt feelings and a need for punishment are the primary factors. The moral masochist is compelled to enter into situations that are disadvantageous for him and in which he is victimized, even though his behavior does not excite sexual pleasure in him or gratify him sexually. The moral masochist is an example of the type of person "who cannot bear success."

In erogenous masochism, sexual pleasure is linked to pain. This form of masochism most certainly represents a perversion of sexual experience.

Feminine masochism is, at least in psychoanalysis, an expression of feminine nature. People who suffer from it place themselves in their fantasies in a "characteristically female situation" (Freud [1924] 1963). By this is generally meant the passive bearing of a person who experiences particular pleasure in serving and self-sacrifice. This pleasure in suffering may, but need not, have a sexual component. Although the distinction between erogenous and feminine masochism is not fully explained by psychoanalytic theory, Freud nonetheless held that women could not enjoy sexual intercourse without the pressure of masochistic suffering.

To characterize this form of masochism as feminine is the result of a common prejudice, for according to clinical experience, so-called feminine masochism is also found in men. This contradiction is supposedly solved by the theory of bisexuality—that is, it is assumed that bisexuality plays a role in the psychic development of all human beings—

except that what is regarded as natural in women is held to be a perversion in men.

If it is true that all women are masochistic either by upbringing or by nature, then all women would also have to be especially rich in fantasy. This would be the logical consequence, at least, if those psychoanalysts are correct who assume that people with a meager fantasy life are not inclined to masochism. But things are not quite so simple, as experience has taught us. Just as psychoanalysts learn to distinguish between symptomatic neurosis and character neurosis, they must also be able to differentiate between masochistic fantasies, masochistic symptoms, and masochistic personality. In a masochistic personality, as in all character neuroses, fantasy life is usually considerably curtailed; inflexibly self-sacrificing postures in women are as a rule linked to an inhibition of their fantasy life. One must also recognize that female patients with fantasies of rape only very rarely experience any pleasure in the realization of their fantasies, as is often falsely claimed.

Sexually stimulating fantasies of rape and denigration can be observed more frequently in women than in men. From more careful observations of such fantasies, it may be seen, however, that qualitatively different processes are involved here; actual rape is almost never perceived as pleasurable. Indeed, it is often accompanied by lasting psychological damage. Fantasized and real rapes cannot be equated. Fantasies of rape are neither as brutal nor as devoid of sympathetic understanding as real ones. In contrast to actual rape, they do not leave one helpless. On the contrary, a person who fantasizes, far from being a victim, is rather the creator and controller of the situation created in fantasy.

Such fantasies can thus serve the purpose of converting

passively experienced oppression into controllable situations, and converting unpleasure into pleasure. Even so,
fantasies about rape can also produce the feeling of being
the slave of one's own fantasies. Then fantasies no longer
serve the purpose of controlling emotional situations, but
control the person who fantasizes. The fact that so many
masochistic fantasies appear in women might be traced
back to centuries of social and familial oppression. Helplessness can no longer be overcome in a stepwise fashion
when fantasies elude one's own ego and its control.

However, when women report fantasies of passive sexual submission to the analyst, it frequently happens that
mixed with the feeling of shame there is an underlying
feeling of triumph that with the help of their fantasies they
are in control of themselves and their potential for pleasure. On the other hand, many women have feelings of
fear, guilt, and shame with respect to their sexuality, above
all when they take the initiative in bringing about and
experiencing sexual excitement. In their opinion, apparently, sexuality should be induced only by the man.

A woman's identification with the role stereotype of the
weak and dependent woman is accompanied by the need
to see the man as a powerful figure, one who offers help
in life and is the focus of life. For some women, erotic
submission serves the purpose of gaining influence over
the man, and thus sharing in his power.

Psychoanalysts frequently accuse feminists of regarding
masochistic needs, fantasies, and forms of behavior as the
result exclusively of social circumstances, that is, of the
patriarchal structures of dominance that determine the
relationship between the sexes. In so doing, according to
the psychoanalysts, feminists underestimate the psychic

consequences of differing sexual characteristics and somatic feelings that must of necessity influence sexual behavior.

The research of Stoller (1968) and others has demonstrated that sexual identity does not develop solely from the psychic processing of anatomy and physiology but is instead fundamentally dependent on how a child has learned to view itself on the basis of its upbringing and the attitudes of its environment, even if these experiences do not correspond to its biological sex. Since girls born without a vagina and boys lacking a penis, as well as blind children, develop in accordance with the sex attributed to them at birth, the knowledge of the anatomical difference between the sexes cannot have the great psychological significance that Freud attributed to it. As has already been noted, according to Stoller, a child's gender-specific self-determination takes place largely in accordance with the sex assigned to it at birth.

More recently, several psychoanalytic authors (Kleeman, 1976; Stoller, 1968) have emphasized that cognitive knowledge, that is learned experience, contributes to the formation of sexual identity. According to this view, the effect of the identification is only secondary, for otherwise it could not be explained why, for example, a young boy whose primary figures of identification are female still clearly feels himself at about three years of age to be a boy. That he does so is said to be the consequence of numerous behavioral instructions and standards of conduct that tell him that he is regarded as a boy. Psychologically this is believed to exert greater psychic influence than does primary identification with female figures.

In my view there is also a danger here of simplifying

complex psychic mechanisms. Identification with female figures and the internalization of security-providing maternal roles have a generalized structuring effect on a child's psyche, and in no way exclusively in a gender-determining sense. But perhaps the development of sexual identity is more dependent than has heretofore been assumed on whatever gender-specific labeling is in each case applied to the child. Psychoanalysts have repeatedly reported from their clinical practice that having children like his mother is a normal fantasy for a thirteen-year-old boy and does not disturb his feeling of being a boy. Moreover, one should also distinguish between identification with a mother's roles and identification with her body image.

In girls, too, confusion about one's own body image and gender stems from a variety of sources and cannot be traced back exclusively to identification with the attitudes of the mother and her ways of behaving. There is general agreement among psychoanalysts that human drives need to be determined by experiences of deprivation and gratification, that is, shaped by human relationships, to develop a psychic representation. This also means that the specific way a drive develops will depend on the behavior of the parents toward the child, on their conscious and unconscious fantasies and expectations, their child-rearing practices, cognitive guidance, and so on. Psychoanalysts have recognized ever more clearly the enormous potential of drives to adapt and change. Destructiveness, whether directed at oneself or at others, depends—as does the capacity for love—on the quality of early object relations; these are in turn conditioned by social role expectations and methods of child rearing and by the fantasies these inspire.

Thanks to their maternal models, many women from an early age see their life's goal as being loved by a man, loving him, admiring him, serving him, adapting to him, and raising his children in maternal self-sacrifice. Even today, heterosexual love is often urged upon women as the sole meaning of life. The inevitable consequence of such ideals, forced on women and internalized from childhood, is the development of a "female masochism." Freud too was thoroughly aware of this.

For Freud, the husband "inherits" his wife's original relationship to her mother, that is, the powerful man is put in the position of the powerful mother. A relationship of lifelong dependence between two people, in which one dominates and the other is dominated, is typical of the sadomasochistic relationship; a girl has an even harder time in breaking out of it than a boy because girls are not as encouraged to develop a need for separation, the childhood period of spite and "no-saying," and thus the necessary dissolution of an exclusively dyadic relationship. Separation anxieties are especially strong in girls, but their need to merge with another person usually also causes them anxieties, since it further intensifies feelings of helplessness that were experienced in the symbiotic unity with the mother. A boy is encouraged to turn to the father, to identify with him, and to not be a "mama's boy." For a girl, the mother frequently remains a self object, one that she begins to hate because the necessary distance could never be established.

The psychoanalyst Anni Reich (1953) spoke of narcissistic object choice in women who are inclined to a strong unconscious overestimation of all things male; in such women the man of their choice is meant to make up for their own inadequacy. Separation from a partner who serves to restore an ego experienced as inadequate will then necessarily be experienced as unbearable and to be avoided at all costs. The economic dependence from which a woman in our society suffers (particularly when she has children or is the first to lose her job in times of rising unemployment) is often aggravated to the point of intolerability owing to her psychic dependence. When divorce means not only economic insecurity but in addition a form of loss of self, a woman must prevent it with every means at her disposal. Masochistic forms of behavior are the inevitable consequence.

Freedom is always limited by consideration for others. But when a girl is brought up even in early childhood to show exceptional consideration and to accommodate to others, her freedom is particularly restricted. Excessive dependence inevitably awakens hatred against the person on whom one is dependent. This in turn causes anxiety, so that the feelings of hatred must be warded off by masochistic types of behavior, leading to sadomasochistic relationships. The more dependent a child—and later the adult—is, and the more entirely reliant the child is on the dyadic relationship, the more probably sadomasochistic forms of relationships become, that is, relationships in which the need for domination and being dominated determine the interpersonal situation.

Due to the diversity of links between reality and fantasy found in human beings, it is necessary to distinguish masochistic fantasies of needing to be punished from masochistic character traits. If women do indeed show exaggeratedly self-sacrificing behavior—exemplified by the wife as the humble servant, the tendency of the mother to be always available to everyone in the family (through which the other family members remain dependent and infantile)—then such masochistic character traits are the result of false ideals that our culture has forced on women for centuries. But in the end these character traits have earned women more scorn than admiration. They represent generations-old chains of identification that are not so easily done away with. The struggle for new ego ideals is unavoidable; women's efforts to make conscious the unconscious motives behind their own behavior and to overcome their feelings of being, as it were, by their very nature inferior to men will lead to new orientations and new forms of behavior.

Moral masochists' unconscious need for punishment and their tendency to seek out situations detrimental to themselves are found in equal proportions in both sexes. The roots of such behavior are to be found in early childhood. The mother of the first years of childhood, experienced as omnipotent, is made responsible for unavoidable disappointments by both sexes and, in consequence, hated. But since she is at the same time loved, and not only children but adults as well are unconsciously dependent on her, this hatred must be repressed. Anxiety-ridden guilt feelings develop in reaction, surfacing in the life of the moral masochist as a need for punishment.

Men experience sexually stimulating masochistic fantasies as particularly shameful; even more than women, they feel themselves the helpless victims of these fantasies and less as their creators. Evidently they are much more afraid than women of losing their sexual identity when they permit themselves fantasies of being raped. They experience such fantasies as perverse. But it is known that men are capable of using their masochistic fantasies and attitudes creatively, as for example in the cases of the writers Proust and Kafka. The various biographers of Proust all agree that following an evening with a friend, he was in the habit of spending a sleepless night, analyzing everything that had been said or left unsaid that evening in the most minute detail and writing his conversational partner long letters about the offenses he had been dealt during the course of the evening. Important segments of Proust's works were derived from the reworking of such experiences. Proust also wrote detailed beating scenes involving sadomasochistic homosexuals and the psychic processing of such episodes. It may even be said that sadomasochistic fantasies of omnipotence conjured up by the antiheros in Kafka's works compensated for their victims' powerlessness, and surely served the same purpose to their creator. Neither Proust nor Kafka was able to free himself from a lifelong Oedipal mother fixation.

When hatred in the relationship with the mother is denied and one makes oneself responsible for every disappointment with her in order to overcome the feeling of being a helpless victim, then the ground is laid for the development of masochistic forms of behavior. The traumatic effects of narcissistic injuries in early childhood are compensated for in that the masochist directs them against himself (see Eidelberg 1934).

Role expectations of women have been considerably transformed over the course of this century. Freud, according to whom a small girl desires a child from her father as a substitute for her genital inferiority, regarded it as obvious that the wish for sexual intercourse and the wish for children should be seen as a unit. This corresponded to the status of women at the time. For women today this unity no longer exists. Clinical experience shows that masochistic types of behavior in women, like hysterical symptoms, are subject to transformation as times change. Such masochistic behavior forms represent complex psychic responses to social phenomena and the methods of child rearing that correspond to them. To see a female ideal in masochistically self-sacrificing behavior, in accordance with traditional value norms, seems absurd to us today. Psychic masochism is unimaginable without the other side of the coin, that is, psychic sadism. Analysts are thoroughly familiar with the passive aggression of masochistic women, who are inclined to behave in a reproachful manner and either incite guilt feelings in others by their self-sacrifice and humble bearing or keep them in a state of permanent dependence. Any sensitive person who is not wholly deformed by his culture will prefer disagreement and self-assertiveness even in women to behavior of this sort.

II

Anti-Semitism– A Male Disease?

ANTI-SEMITISM IS a social disease; it is one of many forms of the irrational solidification of prejudices. But not all anti-Semitism is the same. Anti-Semitism has assumed many shapes and been used for a variety of purposes over the course of the centuries. Not until the end of the eighteenth century, following the French Revolution, did "classical" religious anti-Semitism abate; for Jews, this meant the end of the Middle Ages.

The kind of anti-Semitism that was used for principally political purposes first became virulent in Germany around 1880. The court chaplain Adolf Stoecker and the historian Heinrich von Treitschke made names for themselves in this connection. Treitschke coined the saying "the Jews are our misfortune." Modern anti-Semitism, which under Hitler employed primarily racist arguments, differs substantially from the religious anti-Semitism of the Middle Ages.

As long as the reproaches leveled at Jews had a religious content and they were accused of having killed the Son of God, Jews could escape persecution by being baptized as Christians. Racist anti-Semitism offers no such possibility of evasion; in it the "flaw" lies in the "blood" of the race, which must be blotted out. This led ultimately to Hitler's mass murder, to the "final solution" of the "Jewish question."

Racist anti-Semitism should not be directly equated with racial discrimination, however, for attacks against Jews are always linked to cultural anti-Semitism. In the latter, the particular culture of the Jews and its difference from that of the host country—chosen voluntarily or under duress—becomes at the same time an object of persecution. In Western Christian countries, Jews were frequently regarded as strangers because they clung to their religion, their customs, and their language, emphasized their differentness, and thus in the eyes of their persecutors denigrated the religion, traditions, and customs of their Christian surroundings. Jews living in the Diaspora were at the same time a part of the culture of the country in which they lived. To be foreign, to seclude themselves or be forced into closed ghettos, and at the same time to be tied to Western Christian culture led to an entirely different sort of racism than that directed against clearly foreign cultures, such as those of the Negroes, Mongols, Indians, and so on with whom no direct rivalries existed, since as minorities in European countries they have played only a subordinate role, and for only a brief while.

Anti-Semitism has as we know nothing to do with reality. Xenophobia can also develop without the presence of foreigners in one's country. But these diseases of projection do not become virulent and dangerous until destructive aggressions are directed against an actually present minority. All diseases of prejudice consist in projections and displacements of individual impulses that one refuses to acknowledge. The weakest in a country always become the victims of the projection of people's own repressed and despised qualities, wishes, and feelings. In the latter, the particular culture of the Jews and its difference from that of the host country—chosen voluntarily or under duress—becomes at the same time an object of persecution.

The political purposes served by anti-Semitism and hostility toward foreigners are largely similar. Both are used as lightning rods when social circumstances call for change, but revolutionary impulses need to be curbed and steered into alternative undertakings. For this purpose, the czarist police invented the notorious "Protocols of the Elders of Zion," which was used to justify anti-Semitic pogroms in czarist Russia.

We frequently find that inflammatory writings serve to create scapegoats or to distract attention from deplorable states of affairs. From a psychological point of view, anti-Semitism is a displacement, one that requires rationalization; still, it is astonishing that the aforementioned "Protocols" and similar obvious forgeries were accepted without criticism and regarded as truth by many, including educated people, far into the twentieth century (see Silbermann, 1981).

Just which classes of society are particularly susceptible to anti-Semitism is a question that has been repeatedly pursued. Fetscher (1965) agreed with Engels ([1890] 1953) that anti-Semitism was above all a reaction of the petite bourgeoisie class, which saw its existence threatened by the development of industrialism and capitalism. The petit bourgeois equated Jews with the financial activities of the banks and stock exchanges, and saw them as the concrete representatives of capitalistic economic developments that were wholly incomprehensible to them and eroding their way of life.

The political misuse of anti-Semitism, as well as its psychological and economic causes, are complex. If a Jewish professor, doctor, or lawyer is rejected by his gentile colleagues because he is a rival, it is a different situation from a farmer who vilifies Jews as moneylenders, or a petit bourgeois who feels threatened by capitalism and associates this threat with Jews.

What are the intrapsychic motives for anti-Semitism? There are not many psychoanalytic works dealing with the psychology of anti-Semites. Along with the essays in *Anti-Semitism: A Social Disease,* edited by Ernst Simmel (1964), those in Loewenstein's *Christians and Jews. A Psychoanalytic Study* (1951) are the best known. In 1960, F. Schupper (1962) gave a series of lectures on the subject at the Berlin Psychoanalytic Institute. In 1962, a symposium organized and introduced by Alexander Mitscherlich (Mitscherlich et al. 1962) was held in Wiesbaden on "The Psychological and Social Preconditions for Anti-Semitism." Psychoanalytic contributions included those by Béla Grunberger and Martin Wangh.

Even Freud grappled with religious anti-Semitism in his famous essay "Moses and Monotheism" ([1939] 1963). He saw the psychological basis for Christians' incessantly repeated accusations against Jews ("in Christ you killed our God") in a displacement of patricidal wishes onto the Jews. Nor can jealousy and sibling rivalry be overlooked in anti-Semitism, since the Jewish people saw themselves as God's first-born and favorite sons. Furthermore, according to Freud, that Jews are circumcised is experienced unconsciously as castration. It is strange and incites fear; but it also leads to Jews' being despised. Freud recognized religious anti-Semitism as an expression of sibling rivalry and envy. We find the same psychic defensive measures in racist anti-Semitism, which represents in addition a defensive system against incestuous wishes and disruptions of self-esteem. In characterizing Jews as bad and worthy of destruction, one can project all evil onto them and allow free rein to feelings of envy.

Together with Freud, most psychoanalytic authors (see Fenichel 1940; Menninger 1938) saw anti-Semitism in individuals as the consequence of unresolved Oedipal conflicts. In their investigations, however, the authors confined themselves to the psychosexual development of men. What psychic conflicts cause women to become anti-Semites is a question that has not yet been pursued in any great detail in either psychoanalytic or sociological investigations. Projections of hatred for the father, displacement of incestuous wishes onto Jews ("profanation of the race"), aggressions of rivalry, and so forth—such unconscious motives for the development of anti-Semitism are relevant primarily to the male psyche.

The development of anti-Semitism is also regarded by psychoanalysts as the result of a superego deformation. The superego of the anti-Semite is not made up of internalizations of human objects and relationships, but has been more or less trained (Grunberger 1962; Wangh 1962). For such a superego, which knows only external prohibitions and obligations, what counts above all is power— that of an individual, or of a group, or of a nation. For such a person, moral contents and values play far less of a role.

Internalization of the father's commandments and prohibitions, with the help of which the Oedipal conflict is brought to an end, is not achieved in such cases. Rather, fear of the father's power persists in its primitive form, thus determining the behavior of the anti-Semite. The Oedipal failure of the small boy, that is the nonfulfillment of his sexual desires for his mother, is not attributed to his own sexual immaturity and his relationship with the mother but remains fixed in the unconscious of the adult as being the result of a powerful paternal rivalry. The outcome is a severe narcissistic injury, a wound to the soul that cannot be healed. In order to be able to live with this wound, defensive mechanisms of projection and displacement are activated that in the anti-Semite are focused on the Jews. Thus Grunberger (1962) wrote of the anti-Semite:

If the projection onto the Jews is successful, he has created a Manichean paradise for himself: from now on, all evil is to be found on one side [where the Jew dwells], and all good in the other, his own. . . . His ego ideal is of a narcissistic nature, and gratification is in accordance with a wholly narcissistic integrity which he has achieved via projection onto the Jews . . . Moreover, we know that the unusual adroitness whereby Hitler was able to win over the German people had to do with making Jews responsible for the military defeat of 1918, thus healing the terrible narcissistic injury of the German people, who had been so proud of their army.

Frenkel-Brunswik, and others who contributed to a volume of investigations into the authoritarian personality edited by Theodor Adorno (1950), came to the conclusion that the anti-Semite is frequently inclined to idealize his parents. When the age-appropriate deidealization of the parents does not take place during puberty, there is a considerable disturbance in a person's sense of reality. Parents who present themselves as ideals to their children into puberty and thereafter and who do not permit their children to perceive them in a more or less realistic manner, inhibit their psychological maturation. A person who is unable to face his own reality is usually also incapable of perceiving social reality. The anti-Semite seems constantly to deny reality.

Martin Wangh (1962) offered the hypothesis that the youthful followers of Hitler, who were infants and small children during the years from 1914 to 1918 and so had grown up without a father, reacted to the economic calamity at the end of the 1920s by regressing. The plight of the mothers, left to cope alone during the war years, had thrown them into a state of anxious tension that they transmitted to their children, disrupting the establishment of stable, security-providing object relationships. Since the sons were alone with their mothers for years, their Oedipal complex was intensified and hence their castration anxiety as well. A "splitting" developed: The absent father was glorified, and negative feelings with regard to him were imputed to the enemy. A victorious father can be more easily accepted by a son upon his return than a vanquished, "worthless" father, who is nonetheless experienced as a rival. Such a "worthless" father not only triggers feelings of triumph in his son but deals a severe narcissistic injury to the child as well, since the father is a part of his own self. In summation: The anxieties communicated by the mother, Oedipal guilt, the narcissistic injury resulting from a deidealized father who nevertheless resumed his place at the mother's side as a rival—these were conflicts that were difficult to master. Again the defense mechanisms of displacement and projection were invoked: It was not the father or oneself who was guilty, but rather the Jew to whom guilt for all defeats was attributed; he could be made into an outsider, then despised without fear, and persecuted. Wangh (1962) expressed the fear that a time might soon come again when the young people who had been damaged by the war and the postwar period would grasp for defensive mechanisms similar to those employed in the wake of the First World War. We would then be faced by a new wave of intense anti-Semitism.

"Circumcision is the symbolic substitute for the castration which the primal father once inflicted upon his sons in the plenitude of his absolute power, and whoever accepted that symbol was showing by it that he was prepared to submit to the father's will, even if it imposed the most painful sacrifice on him," wrote Freud ([1939] 1963, 23:230). Bettelheim ([1954] 1962), who investigated the puberty rites of primitive people, came to different conclusions. He believed that both penis envy in girls and castration anxiety in boys were overemphasized in psychoanalysis, and that the much deeper psychological layer of envy of the mother, particularly in boys, was neglected. Penis envy in a society in which men play the predominant role can be expressed much more openly than men's feelings of envy of women, which conflict with social norms; such feelings are generally regarded as anomalous at least, if not perverse.

Psychoanalytic authors such as Melanie Klein ([1932] 1975) and Gregory Zilboorg ([1944] 1979) pointed out many years ago that the femininity complex (envy of women) in men is much less well explained and more mysterious than the castration complex (envy of men) in women. These authors regarded a man's envy of women as phylogenetically older and more fundamental than penis envy.

Bettelheim saw some primitive puberty rites as a socially recognized way of representing the feminine traits and wishes of men, of being able to fulfill them symbolically and thus being better able to cope with unconscious hatred and envy toward women than "enlightened" man in the Western Hemisphere can.

Men in our culture, who have no such ritualized forms of expressing their fantasies, can displace repressed hatred toward the father and envy of the mother onto the Jews. The question thus arises whether, when, and what sort of rituals might create an antidote to anti-Semitism.

Such other analysts as Fenichel, Wangh, and Grunberger also see the repression of unconscious animosity toward an omnipotent mother as an additional important factor in anti-Semitism; her fear-inspiring aspects, displaced onto the Jews, become "Jewish uncanniness." Since Jews belong to a minority despised by many, every imaginable negative behavior pattern and characteristic can be attributed to them without risking either fear or guilt.

If the psychoanalytic view that women rarely harbor patricidal wishes, are not particularly plagued by rivalry with respect to their first-born sons, and suffer less than men from castration and incest anxieties is correct, then what repressed feelings and needs, psychoanalytically speaking, are they displacing and projecting when they become anti-Semites?

Both sexes appear to share intense feelings of underlying hatred and envy toward the mother of early childhood, who is experienced as omnipotent and phallic—feelings that can later be displaced onto less dangerous scapegoats in order to avoid excessive anxiety. To this may be added the fact that women too are afraid of their incestuous wishes because they fear the mother's rage and are afraid of losing her love.

Jews have always been both a familiar and an unfamiliar element in Western Christian culture; for many non-Jews, they held the attraction of the forbidden. For some women, the desire to become involved with a Jewish man was therefore as tempting, but at the same time as anxiety-provoking, as incestuous wishes with regard to the father. The repression of such wishes, and their projection onto others, may on occasion have contributed to women's defaming Jews as desecrators of the race, or, as the historian Treitschke averred, as "our misfortune." Even so, such psychological attempts to explain the development of anti-Semitic prejudices in women are hardly convincing.

Perhaps anti-Semitism in women could be better understood with the help of psychoanalytic theories about the development of the superego. Anti-Semites are generally inclined to deny reality, as mentioned, and exhibit a substantially disturbed superego. This "anti-Semitic superego" may be distinguished from the typically "female" superego portrayed by Freud. The "weak" superego of women is regarded as the result of their lack of castration anxiety; they are said therefore to have experienced no emotional constraint comparable to that of men to internalize parental prohibitions and commandments. "This variation [that is, the construction of a superego through internalized parental prohibitions] appears, much more than in boys, to be the product of upbringing and an external intimidation that threatens with the loss of love" (Freud [1924] 1963).

Toward the end of his life, Freud explained that the seduction fantasies of his patients that he had reported were not directed at the father but at the mother. "The pre-Oedipal phase in women gains an importance which we have not attributed to it hitherto" ([1931] 1963). According to this theory, women remain largely fixated on an incestuous relationship to the father or on a love-hate relationship with the mother.

But anti-Semitism involves emotional problems other than simply unresolved ties and ambivalences with regard to the parents. It is characterized above all by a tendency toward crude projections, a tendency that interferes with the anti-Semite's capacity to apprehend reality adequately. With regard to the demands of their drives, anti-Semites are uncritical and blind.

In our culture, warded-off anality in the form of strictures and moral sadism is found more prominently in men than in women. Women, it appears, are usually better able to tolerate guilt feelings and an element of disorder. They are protected against "law-and-order" fetishism by their "weak" superegos. Thus they are less inclined than men to denial and repression of their feelings.

If the superego of women, more oppressed by fear of loss of love than by castration anxiety, is different from that of men and different from the superego of the massively projecting anti-Semite, characterized as it is by anal-sadistic traits and "sphincter morality" (order, cleanliness, obedience, etc.), how can it be explained that women too conform to the attitudes formed by a male-dominated society? For they are inclined to assume the political and social prejudices of their fathers, brothers, and husbands. From this it may be concluded that women fall prey to anti-Semitism less as a result of their own castration anxieties, psychic conflicts, and projections than as a consequence of their identification with male prejudices. This tendency to conform in turn has to do with women's great fear of loss of love, a fear that was described even by Freud. This fear is first experienced with respect to the mother—a mother who in turn habitually conforms to male society for the same reason.

Films about the Third Reich remind us graphically of the now almost forgotten behavior of German women during that time, how uncritically they accepted their second-class status and how enthusiastically they approved of the "morality" and perverse ideals of the Nazi era. They complied devotedly with the contradictory demands made of them during the Nazi era—playing the roles of the little wife in the kitchen who was supposed to bear sons for the Führer, of cadre leaders, of munitions workers, or even of concentration camp guards. Many were prepared to go along with all that was asked of them.

Thus very few women in Germany distanced themselves from the anti-Semitism of the time; at any rate, resistance on the part of women to the dictates of public opinion issued by the Nazis has seldom been recorded. Women are naturally inclined, like all weak and oppressed elements of a society, to identify with the aggressor, to submit themselves to his opinions and to share them, even—or precisely—when they themselves are thereby denigrated.

Some psychoanalysts—as, through the centuries, philosophers and literati (including Aristotle, Schopenhauer, Gottfried Keller, Strindberg, and many others)—have denied women's possession of a stable morality and the capacity for objectivity. In so doing, they obviously overlook that the capacity to form objective judgments does not amount to much in men either. To be sure, men may have learned to better isolate their emotions and thereby appear more "objective." But this is linked to the fact that compulsively neurotic traits linked to emotional repression appear more frequently in men. To characterize such neurotic tendencies as morality is erroneous (see Schafer 1974).

Psychoanalytic theory regards castration anxiety in men and fear of loss of love in women as the central motifs. Castration anxiety, which has to do with one's own person and its destruction, is thus to be characterized as narcissistic. In fear of loss of love, in contrast, relationships to other human beings remain of the greatest importance. This too influences the formation of the psychic authority of the superego.

The development of the superego is not to be equated with the development of moral capability. A superego made up of infantile anxieties and guilt feelings, anal-sadistic impulses and their warding off, is an irrational, rigid, corruptible authority, one susceptible to "training." Women's greater orientation toward objects ought to enable them to construct a less rigid, less emotion-repressing superego, and to develop a morality that is more loving, more flexible, and more humane than that of men—not a "weak" superego, but a different one, a superego more oriented to the preservation of relationships with closely associated people.

The more psychoanalysis had to respond to the variety of clinical experience, the more complex its theory became. Today psychoanalytic theory encompasses more than just the laws of a drive-determined, unconscious psychic dynamic; it proceeds from the assumption that all aspects of development, including those determined by drives, are influenced by object relationships with other people and by learning.

Freud revised and added to his theory several times during the course of his life. It was clear to him that in addition to the vicissitudes of penis envy, a girl's relationship with her mother had a profound influence on her later development (see Freud [1931] 1963). In addition to hatred resulting from an early total dependence on the mother and the corresponding guilt feelings, an erotically tinged love relationship to the mother became unmistakable in girls.

At the same time, the small girl already identifies with her mother in early childhood. This primary identification corresponds to the dependence but also offers a way out of that dependence as the child's emotional world undergoes a step-by-step maturation process.

Thus it is important to distinguish among the various consequences of early-childhood dependence: On the one hand, we find defense mechanisms and reaction formations such as hatred, rejection, denial, refusal, repression, defiance, masochism, and much more; on the other hand, children internalize positive capabilities of reality-mastering and anxiety-alleviating, consoling maternal functions that are of central importance in the formation of the child's ego. A child's identification with the aggressor, in the sense of learning to say no, can, according to René Spitz, be one of the most important preconditions for a person's development of self-sufficiency, and has other aspects besides brainwashing and uncritical conformity. A boy is forced to deidealize his mother earlier than a girl; he is expected to be "manly." This type of "manliness" is frequently accompanied by the aforementioned disruption of his emotional world. The consequences of such early interruptions of the internalization of maternal attitudes and functions can often be observed in adult men, for example, when they repress their feelings in order to appear objective and unemotional—that is "manly" as dictated by their upbringing.

Although both sexes identify in the beginning with a mother who is experienced as omnipotent, young girls often appear less anxious and helpless than boys even during this early developmental period; in girls the gradual internalization of maternal functions is less disrupted from the outside than it is in boys. Whatever a boy is able to preserve of his internalizations will help him later to behave in a "fatherly" fashion toward his own children. Even if fear of loss of love does often aggravate an unfortunate tendency to conform on the part of women, it also promotes the openly displayed need to be loved, the humanity of a person, more than the more narcissistically centered orientation of men toward masculinity.

If it is correct that anti-Semitism is primarily a superego disturbance, then it has much more to do with the characteristic development of the male superego than that of the female. Women's superego structures do not predestine them to anti-Semitism. Their dependence on the recognition of their environment, on prevailing male value orientations, may nonetheless cause them to adopt current prejudices.

Only women who learn to develop and defend their own systems of values can contribute to the prevention of inhumane disease like anti-Semitism, as well as all other forms of discrimination. With the strengthening of women's position in society, the dominance of men equipped with rigid, compulsory, narcissistic, emotion-repressing superegos would be weakened.

Anti-Semitism is, as we have said, a social disease, that is a disease of a particular society and not of the individual. But if, on the other hand, anti-Semitism is connected to typically male development, it may be concluded that the emotional makeup of the individual man and the manner of his upbringing and his internalization of parental prohibitions and behavior contribute to making illnesses of prejudice chronic.

In my opinion, there is such a thing as male and female anti-Semitism. Anti-Semitism in women develops by means of conformity to male prejudices rather than as a result of gender-specific development and upbringing. But in seeking to understand these differences in the formation of prejudice, we still know too little about what distinguishes the psyches of men and women so profoundly and what causes them such seemingly insuperable difficulties in understanding one another.

Jews are especially suited as the enemy within—within a country or within a society—an enemy that both belongs and does not belong to the family. All family problems and all conflicts between the sexes can be displaced onto them without great difficulty. If there are no longer any

Jews present—and the structure of existing relations between the sexes remains unchanged—it becomes necessary to invent a substitute for them. Only the "descent
into hell of self-recognition" (Kant) can liberate us from
dangerous tendencies to projection and displacement, and
alleviate disturbances of empathy existing between the
sexes. The precondition for this is an analysis and critique
of the prevailing "reality principle."

12

Patriarchs in a Fatherless Society

WE LIVE IN a time of diverse and changing values. The so-called fatherless society, which would seem increasingly to be taking shape, is welcomed by some and rejected by others. Many observers have seen it as a step forward in human relationships, others as the dissolution of cultural conventions. But what is a fatherless society?

In a society defined by men, we continue to find ourselves surrounded by hierarchies. In economics, in politics, in government and religious institutions, men still set the tone. Women play only a minor role, if any at all. If patriarchal structures in the family have changed considerably by comparison with previous centuries, they have not disappeared there either. So why do so many today speak of a fatherless society?

Alexander Mitscherlich ([1963] 1969) used the term primarily to describe a state of affairs in which the father's daily work has vanished without trace. A disintegration of the father image, he said, had taken place as a consequence of our technical-industrial civilization. With the disappearance of the father's concrete occupational image, the instructional function the father once filled within the family became largely insignificant.

For most people, the state no longer represents paternal authority as it once did. It is shaped by a more or less anonymous circle of technically trained experts and professional politicians. These specialists make up what one might call an elite fraternity. Women play hardly any role whatsoever in this milieu; even today women work almost without exception as salaried employees or in the service professions.

That women continue to allow themselves to be guided by tradition in their choice of profession can surely be traced not only to the fact that, despite intense rivalries among themselves, men continue to banish women from their "men's clubs," but also to the fact that most of the professions once reserved for men now lack any visibility and offer no basis for positive identification.

To be sure, we live in a male-dominated society, but one in which there is little "fatherliness" as an emotional quality, or in the sense of an instructive cultural model. The so-called nuclear family, in which father, mother, and child assume the traditional roles laid down for them, appears to be disintegrating faster than we had previously realized. It is no longer the father who plays the leading role within the family, but the mother. It is to her that children turn with their desires and concerns. Though this naturally arouses the jealousy of the father, and he feels left out, he is nonetheless inclined to experience his children as a burden and refer them quickly to their mother if they should happen to demand his attention. He seems in many cases to be at least dimly aware of how far removed he is from himself, his feelings, and his daily physical experience. This suspicion and the concomitant fear of having to confess his failings openly contribute to making him into a difficult father and a difficult husband, one who can not tolerate mutualism. He then takes out his frustrations with himself and his envy of his wife on both her and his children.

The underlying envy of men for women has already been discussed. A man defends himself against a woman's gaining a singular significance in his life out of his own envy and jealousy, emotions that stem from early childhood, when the mother is experienced as all-powerful. To change relationships frequently—thus turning women into articles of consumption—is a characteristically male form of defense against an original hatred of women and dependence on them.

A mother is typically forced into an overly nurturing role, and the result is that all the family members, including the husband, retain or develop childish forms of behavior. A variety of maternal roles exist in our society and do not necessarily preclude one another. Often such differing postures are combined: On the one hand, the woman assumes her appointed role as omnipotent mother in order to compensate for her feelings of helplessness stemming from childhood and her feelings of inferiority at being shut out of male society; on the other hand, she clings to the role of a child in need of support, idealizes her husband (as once she had idealized her father), and expects him to be protective and superior. Of course we also increasingly encounter independent women who toil to hold their own both professionally and socially; but within the family such women too often continue to play the role of the self-sacrificing mother and servant.

Even so, unease with all that was once understood as

"manliness" can be observed on all sides. The father has been increasingly called into question as the head of the family, not only as a result of a growing awareness of the central importance of the mother-child relationship but also owing to the growth of a vital women's movement. In Germany, two lost wars and, above all, the collapse of the Nazi regime contributed to a rapid devaluation of the father image. Hymnic glorification of the father has been succeeded by repudiation of authoritarian paternal rule and an ever more widespread hatred of the father.

The rejection of the father therefore has to do not only with his invisibility as an occupational model but also with the now crumbling forms of authoritarian child rearing, once dominated by the relationship between father and son, that above all else kindled fear and aggression. The father of the ruling class of the previous century was a paradigm of order-giving authority, accustomed to obedience and punishing without hesitation. He was not permitted to admit loving feelings toward his son (to the extent that they were present at all); to do so was to be regarded as derelict in his duty.

Only since the authoritarian father image has disappeared as an ideal for young people and lost almost all its attraction have attempts been made to redefine "fatherhood" (see Mitscherlich and Mitscherlich 1983, among others). Many have lost sight of what fatherhood might actually be, if they ever had a picture of it to begin with. The authority of a "good father" is based not on commands but on protective functions, on personal capability, on being able to establish empathetic contact with his children and, above all, with the mother, and on being able to gain respectability as a model for the kind of child rearing we have outlined.

In contrast, paternal claims to respect and obedience are not as a rule confirmed by the actual behavior of the father nor by the respectability of his professional occupation. The child does not know the father in his work, is unaware of his standing among his fellow workers, whether he conducts himself with self-confidence or is oppressed and unhappy in the workplace. At home the family often experiences him as dependent, both emotionally and factually, and at the same time as a hypercritical and disparaging authority who unjustly asserts himself.

With the help of two examples—I shall call the patients involved Erich and Doris—I would like to sketch the role of the father in family relationships.

Erich came to me for treatment for depression and psychosomatic symptoms. He had been born during the Second World War and had seen his father only sporadically during the first years of his life. Erich's mother had assumed responsibility for her two children, apparently with pride and care as long as the father was absent. Erich considered himself the most sensitive of his siblings and believed himself particularly loved by the mother. He in turn loved her and felt very dependent on her. As a result of his numerous dermatological ailments and on the advice of doctors, his mother began tying his hands to the bedframe at night so that he could not hurt himself by scratching. He reacted to this with fear, rage, and helplessness and turned away from his mother for a time; this only aggravated his anxiety. His frequent psychosomatic illnesses, even as an adult, led to the conclusion that the phase of necessary separation from the overly close (though ambivalent) relationship with the mother of early child- hood had not been resolved, as would have been appro- priate for his development.

The father, whose return he had eagerly awaited, soon failed to live up to Erich's expectations and hopes. Erich, like his mother, had idealized him as a hero and could make little headway with the real man, who returned sick and broken from a prisoner-of-war camp and could not control his temper. The pleasant times with his cheerful mother, which he had rarely been forced to share with his sister, were now over. His father was now the focal point, and Erich experienced him as a tyrant who demanded all of his mother's attention for himself.

Despite his disappointment, Erich in the beginning felt a need to win his father's love by any means, to be at his service and fulfill his wishes. But he rarely received any recognition for so doing. Usually he experienced his father as impatient and often brutal as well. In the course of time, Erich turned away from his father but then his almost complete rejection was increasingly answered by his father with punishments and beatings.

Erich never experienced a triangular father-mother-child relationship, in which the father's empathy for both the children and the mother forms a bridge between the var- ious family members; with the help of such a bridge the children slowly learn to empathize with others. The lack of an intimate third person resulted in Erich's being unable to separate himself from the early ambivalent dependence characteristic of the dyadic relationship with the mother; this failure contributed to his chronic psychosomatic dis- turbances. These psychosomatic ailments in turn triggered hypochondriac anxieties and depression.

Erich finally abandoned his emotional relationship with

his father once and for all, even before high school. By then, as far as he knew, Erich felt only fear and hatred toward his father, and he experienced his father's relatively early death as something of a relief. Beneath the surface, as emerged during the analysis, his need for a father who could grant him security and love remained— a father whom he longed for as a liberator from a symbiotic fusion with his mother.

Erich's relationships with women were uniformly difficult. His longing for emotional fusion produced bonding anxieties and simultaneously a feeling of being threatened in his sexual identity. When he nonetheless finally married and had children, he was at pains to be a different sort of father than the one he himself had had. There was no danger of Erich's behaving in an unsympathetic or authoritarian manner; on the contrary, he was inclined to bind his children too much to him. He seemed to be able to empathize with his children more easily than with his wife, since as a result of his desire for fusion, he needed to maintain a distance from her in order to alleviate his fear of loss of identity as a physical male.

Since he had a high ego ideal—that is he made great ethical demands on himself and others—Erich despised his own father, whom he had experienced as lacking in empathy, and who had occasionally committed little dishonesties and self-righteously supported the double standard in the workplace and in the family. Moreover, Erich also scorned many other fathers he had met over the course of his lifetime, including some at the university who had come to terms with society in a similar manner.

A combination of a high ideal of fatherhood and repressed identification with an unrespected and unloved real father—which amounts to a lack of a binding superego in day-to-day matters—often causes young people to withdraw from society and to regard criminal behavior as necessary or even natural, or to attempt to find salvation in sects or cults—that is to look for satisfaction of their idealizations and needs for perfection in order to maintain their denials.

But the lack of a comprehensible and close father image appears to have painful consequences not only for a son's development, but also for that of a daughter. A further example should help to illustrate this point.

Doris sought help because she suffered from a variety of anxieties, an oppressive insecurity, and an inordinate susceptibility to illness. When we look at this young woman's past history, we notice first of all that her earliest childhood remained pleasant and cheerful in her memory, though she had experienced later years as dark and dismal. Her parents' ever more violent quarrels had contributed to this; eventually, they had separated. As so often happens, the father had remained only marginally involved in the family from the very first; while his daughter was still small, he had been completely unable to deal with her. She was, after all, "only" a girl. As she grew older and he felt that he should be able to expect some basic knowledge and a measure of self-assurance from her, he had made clear to her how little she corresponded to his expectations of a cultivated young woman.

Doris had internalized her father's overly critical attitudes to the extent that she became compulsively and severely self-critical. Often she felt at the mercy of a tormenting tendency to self-observation. Her mother had attempted to hold her own against the father and to be a protective shield for the child, but these efforts had been largely unsuccessful. To an extent, the mother had scorned the father, who was not very successful in his career, but she had also subjected herself to his often biting criticism, and had suffered from self-hatred and insecurity.

Doris had studied to be a kindergarten teacher; in the presence of children and young people who turned to her for help, she felt capable of giving and in some measure secure, capabilities she appeared to have acquired from her mother. But Doris had another side as well: With colleagues and people of her own age she could be just as sharp and critical as her father had been with her. She was afraid of becoming like her father, who on the one hand, had been incapable of achieving control over his own life, but who on the other hand moved on the fringes of society owing to his arrogance; he felt himself superior to most people and made this clear. With Doris things were sometimes similar; she was quite aware of her fantasies of superiority and greatness.

Her mother's second marriage had been to a seemingly very well adjusted man, who upon closer examination turned out to be no less insecure than Doris's natural father; the only difference was that he expressed his feelings of worthlessness in an opposite way. The stepfather had adapted himself utterly to small-town life, a milieu in which he felt at home. There, he dared present his new, divorced wife and child with only minor apologies. The result was that mother and daughter had believed that they had to conduct themselves like little gray mice in order not to stand out. The mother, who had managed to put up some resistance to her first husband, had conformed wholly to the prejudices and moral hypocrisies of the environment of her second marriage. At the same time, the role distribution within the family had been such that the father behaved in a weak and dependent manner (as is frequently the case), but the mother—overly nurturing and often beset by an excess of tasks—had attempted to satisfy everyone's needs. Doris's feeling of self-esteem had sunk to nothing; she had believed that she had no choice but to understand herself as a tiresome person who frequently made a negative impression. She had compensated for all these humiliations with fantasies of greatness, wanting above all to become famous.

Doris had felt little protection from her father and had no father image to which she could orient herself. She experienced the first of her fathers as vainglorious and authoritarian, the second as meek and conformist. Both were weak personalities and largely incapable of empathizing with their children, respecting their wives, or allowing a feeling of inner security to develop in their children. Nor could these fathers convey to their children how one learns empathy for others and respect for those who think differently. In such families, people either tend to quarrel violently with each other, or to withdraw depressively; there would seem to be no such thing as discussion, in which people feel they are allowed to be themselves, meet with understanding, and enjoy new experiences with themselves and others.

During the 1960s, there were still violent conflicts between critical, politically interested young people and their parents or parent figures. Often there were violent disputes about past and present values, accompanied by a search for new ideals and models. But the political revolt of students during the late 1960s did not last long.

Political activity among young people in Germany today has turned to new topics and problems; ecological questions are in the forefront, and the peace movement is supported by large portions of the population. But people are far less interested in coming to terms with the Nazi past or in complex historical and theoretical examinations than the youth of the 1960s and 1970s. They are more oriented toward the present; they suffer from the knowledge that the possibility of nuclear war threatens destruction beyond all imagination. For them, the "paternal" state consists of technocrats (with their narrow, specialized interests) and bureaucrats (employees of the administrative machinery who are kept in step by work lacking in substance, by ignorance, and by so-called compulsory specialization). All of this is felt to be particularly painful because it forces us to abandon our faith in progress. A progress that destroys more than it builds, in which the masses have only a passive stake, produces widespread resistance.

Infantile dependency on the state, its bureaucracy, and seemingly objective necessities that prevent people from attaining the freedom to exercise responsibility, awakens embitterment and resignation in many people, feelings that are either conscious or repressed from consciousness. Today, as in the past, young people are presented with an image of an adult who allows apparently senseless processes to occur for the sake of stability and a measure of comfort in their lives—an attitude that thoughtlessly allows free rein to the possibility of incalculable destruction.

But there are signs that more and more people are seeking new forms of thought, new forms of living with one another. Today peevish apathy no longer exhausts itself in fanatic prejudices, in the abuse of alcohol and drugs, or in blind consumerism. Having first infused the student revolution, a will to bring about real change is slowly being expressed through the peace movement, through the creation of ecologically concerned political parties like the Greens, and in associations of like-minded people. Only a relatively small part of the population participated in the student revolt of the 1960s, by comparison with the numbers in the peace movement and in those groups concerned with the environment. Such people are trying to combat ossified traditional ways of thinking about progress and about offensive and defensive military strategies. Frequently those in the peace movement are maligned as regressive, infantile, and distant from reality. It is true that in many, a "regression in the service of the ego" (Kris 1952) does take place. For to become capable of new forms of thought, old roles and identifications must be given up, which leads to a partial dismantling of existing psychological structures, which also, at least initially, occasions regression.

It is dangerous to forget or repress history, to fail to learn from experience. We then cling to outmoded forms of thought, ones that should long since have been made obsolete by progressive insights into reality. Primarily tradition-oriented thought can easily come close to a repetition compulsion. In his discussion of Erik Erikson's notion of identity, H. Lichtenstein (1977) emphasized that only new forms of thought enable people to "make history." Therefore one must reckon with the fact that any new paradigm will have to do without traditional historical consciousness. There is still the problem of whether there can be new paradigms—that is, new forms of thought and knowledge with reference to individual and social roles and structures. Can there be models that are not only plausible in themselves, offering the careful systematization of a Marx or a Freud, but are also capable of evolving and are open to critical objections? To repress historical experiences is surely to go down a blind alley and does not motivate us to undertake more lasting inquiries.

Our opportunities for identification in childhood and youth to a large extent determine the richness and stability of our personality. In the absence of fundamental relationships with people during our first years of life and without the internalization of their functions and forms of behavior, we feel ourselves lacking in orientation and lost in our later relationships with other human beings. But if during the course of further development childhood identifications are not constantly renewed, expanded, and called into question, fixations to early identifications make us incapable of learning and block new experiences of thought and feeling. It would be a good thing if our models, our "fathers" and "mothers," could teach their children not to orient themselves only in accordance with their parents' values, but would permit and encourage their children to say no, to blaze new trails, and to develop new ways of thinking and behaving (see M. Mitscherlich 1978).

The father of centuries past was certainly no model for such an open, flexible way of dealing with others. But in recent times new notions and ideas about fatherliness have begun to make their mark. Men are increasingly willing to share housework, change roles with their wives from time to time, and share the responsibility for raising the children. They refuse to act as models in the sense of an unquestionable authority, for they know all too well that paternal severity that denies its own faults and limitations does not awaken love or encourage a capacity for empathy, but instead results in fear or overly adaptive behavior conditioned by fear that conceals deep-seated aggressions. The behavioral stencils of the personality type produced by authoritarian upbringing quickly fall to pieces when the fear-inducing authority disappears, and their aggressions and sadism are unloaded more or less without inhibition on whatever vulnerable targets can be found.

The wish for new forms of fatherliness is becoming stronger and stronger in the younger generation; rigid defenses against self-criticism are increasingly being called into question. Fatherliness in the sense of an empathetic father, one who assumes responsibility, who no longer falls for clichés of "masculinity," can be observed ever more frequently in private, familial spheres.

In economics and politics, however, it is rare to find such changes as paternal self-criticism or resistance to out-moded authoritarian clichés. In those spheres, authori-tarian father images and elitist fraternities have to a large extent been preserved. Archaic notions of manhood and the double standard continue to dominate wide segments of our society.

Thus, in addition to new forms of fatherhood and changed ideas about what constitutes masculinity, we still find tra-ditional forms of behavior and value judgments both within the family and in society at large. This leads to conflicts and confrontations and causes a climate of misunderstand-ing between the generations. Individuals likewise sense a wide variety of contradictory orientations and behavior patterns within themselves. On the one hand, some men have learned to regard empathy, humaneness, and open-ness toward children, women, and themselves as goals; on the other hand, they are still in the grip of their society's delusions about masculinity, its double standard, its un-critical belief in progress, and its cynicism.

It has often been noted that these contradictory elements of the psychic structure and social ideas of morality inherited from tradition that contrast with a person's own experience can result in psychic stresses that produce multiple personalities. When this happens, people collapse into their component parts and fundamentally cannot understand themselves.

Is there, then, a "fatherless society"? Yes, in business and politics, everywhere where men's clubs, fraternities, "manliness" in the traditional, self-idealizing sense, and the double standard is to be found. Within the family, the authoritarian father has lost his power of attraction for the children. Fathers of this kind are exposed to rejection, indeed often ridicule. People strive for a new form of fatherhood, one that is in many respects similar to what used to be understood as motherhood and has very little to do with authoritarian forms of upbringing. But this in turn of course raises new problems, of both an individual and a social nature.

AFTERWORD

Female Aggression– A Model?

IT WILL HAVE BECOME clear to the reader by now that it is unrealistic to hold up an image of a nonaggressive, peaceable woman against that of an aggressive, bellicose man, in an effort to offer a recipe for solving all social problems and conflicts. Everything we know—including observations from psychoanalysis and psychoanalytic practice—suggests that aggressive potentials are present in both sexes from birth onward and can be awakened at any time. These aggressive potentials are also needed to foster activity and the child's capacity for individuation and self-definition. The difference between the sexes consists exclusively in how drives and aggressive impulses are worked through and expressed; this distinction is, however, of fundamental importance.

In this respect we can establish substantial differences, differences that to a large extent may be explained on the basis of forms and practices of child rearing, that is, on socialization. Obviously, conscious and unconscious methods for the so-called social distribution of labor have been at work for centuries. In social practice, there is a separation into a male mentality of achievement and conquest (with all its well-known and, at present, extreme destructive consequences) on the one hand, and a protective, self-sacrificing, serving mentality for women (also with its unmistakable consequences for the internal and external conduct of life) on the other. If this kind of sadomasochistic relationship between the sexes is linked to pleasure—that is, if men's pleasure in conquering and giving orders is tied to women's pleasure in being dominated and satisfying those who give the orders—then only constantly renewed efforts to make these miserable psychic entanglements conscious can liberate people from them.

It would seem high time to break out of such an external and internal "division of labor" with its disastrous consequences—the destruction of both the outer and the inner world. If we cannot eliminate them, we can at least alleviate them. We will never be able to completely do away with aggression; it is a fundamental part of the human apparatus and does not lead only to destruction; aggression also has a survival function. The capacity of aggression to be transformed is considerable. Fear can be transformed into aggression, aggression into fear. Idealization and hatred can cancel each other out or become fatefully linked to one another. In the recent past in Germany, such a linkage, breaking through every cultural barrier, has led to incalculable destruction.

But in our way of dealing with the internalization and disposal of aggression there is a largely unconscious, one-sided splitting off of certain emotional mechanisms. The dynamics of this are mainly socially determined and—without meaning to underestimate their catastrophically destructive potential—these unconscious dynamics might be displaced, mitigated, and rendered more accessible to self-critical examination. In this undertaking, each sex could help the other. Men should learn to understand that with their projections and aggressiveness toward scapegoats they are perpetuating an age-old ever-worsening destructive cycle that now threatens us with global extinction. And women must come to recognize that in turning their aggression against themselves and so being easily manipulated via their guilt feelings, they not only harm themselves, but help to maintain the fateful cycle of male aggression and flawed idealization. The one is shaped by the other. And if, as is obvious, men derive deep narcissistic gratification from the power and influence they gain through aggression, and if therefore they are unable—or unwilling—to give it up, then women must learn to thwart this age-old ingrained interplay of male pleasure in attacking and destroying and female joy in submitting and sacrificing.

Such changes cannot be accomplished overnight. But the usual time spans in which changes are brought about would seem to be too long when compared with the rapid accumulation of military, social, and ecological potential for destruction that we have witnessed in recent years. It is not just pessimists and prophets of world doom who urge haste upon us; even optimists and those who affirm life are disquieted when they observe the odd contradition between talk of peace in the highest political offices and the ceaseless activity of the arms race. Since the "top men," balanced on their political tightropes, with their clearly self-serving logic of argumentation, are inaccessible to reason and common sense, the public at large, the grass roots, will have to become active in order to avert the fate that looms before us. A particularly important task falls to women: They, the traditionally oppressed ones, appear to be increasingly sensitive to old and new forms of oppression, oppression by technocrats and specialists, oppression by theorists and magicians of specialized knowledge and of all these modern verbal deceptive maneuvers that obscure reality.

Women's heightened sensitivity to all forms of repression, developed despite centuries of enforced pleasure in submission and resignation, needs to be employed more forcefully for the good of us all. It is up to women to change the primary sadomasochistic forms of socialization that lie at the root of relations between the sexes. It is up to women to prevent their male companions from constantly finding scapegoats, whether in private, professional, or political life. It is up to women to withhold their admiration, an admiration that is necessary to preserve this male mentality, from male pretensions of intimidation and self-glorification, the roots of so many violent actions and warlike disputes. Furthermore, women need to reexamine and question their own identification with male ideals and values. But it is also up to women to win for themselves positions that men have monopolized in order to bring to bear their more "peaceable," more reasonable, and more object-related attitudes on many of life's questions. It is up to women to remind themselves of their history and to reflect on their past and present models.

Bibliography

English versions have been listed for all works cited where they could be found. In cases where the publication date differs from the citation date (in parentheses), the discrepancy indicates a translation, or, in a few cases, a more readily available reprinting.

ABELIN, E. L. 1971. The role of the father in the separation-individuation process. In *Separation-individuation, Essays in honor of Margaret Mahler*, ed. J. D. McDevitt and C. F. Settlage, 229–52. New York.

———. 1975. Some further observations and comments on the earliest role of the father. In *International Journal of Psycho-Analysis* 56: 293–302.

ADORNO, TH. W. 1949/50. *The Authoritarian Personality*. New York, 1950.

Balint, M. 1952. *Primary love, and psycho-analytic technique*. London.

———. 1968. The basic fault; therapeutic aspects of regression. London.

Beauvoir, S. de. 1949. *The Second Sex*. New York, 1953.

Bettelheim, B. 1954. *Symbolic wounds; puberty rites and the envious male*. New York, 1962.

———. 1962. *Dialogues with mothers*. New York.

———. 1967. *The empty fortress; infantile autism and the birth of the self*. New York.

Blum, H. P., ed. 1976. *Female psychology: Contemporary psychoan-alytic views* (supp. to *Journal of the American Psychoanalytic Assoc.* 24).

Boehlich, W. 1965. *Der Berliner Antisemitismusstriet.* Frankfurt.

Chasseguet-Smirgel, J., ed. 1964. *Female sexuality; new psychoanalytic views by Janine Chasseguet-Smirgel.* Ann Arbor, 1970.

———. 1964. Feminine Guilt and the Oedipus Complex. In Chasse-guet-Smirgel, 1964a.

———. 1975. Bemerkungen zum Mutterkonflikt, Weiblichkeit und Realitätszerstörung. *Psyche* 29: 805–12.

Chesler, Ph. 1972. *Women and madness.* New York.

———. 1978. *About men.* New York.

Dahmer, H. 1983. Kapitulation vor der "Weltanschauung." *Psyche* 37: 1116–35.

Deutsch, H. 1925. Psychologie des Weibes in den Funktion der Fort-pflanzung (The psychology of women in the reproductive func-tion). *Internationale Zeitschrift für Psychoanalyse* 11: 40–59.

———. 1930. Der feminine Masochismus und seine Beziehung zur Frigidität (Feminine masochism and its relation to frigidity). *Internationale Zeitschrift für Psychoanalyse* 16.

———. 1944. *The psychology of women; a psychoanalytic interpretation by Helene Deutsch.* New York.

———. 1973. *Confrontations with myself: An epilogue.* New York.

Drews, S., and R. Zwiebel. 1978. Entscheidungen und ihre Psycho-dynamik in der "Lebensmitte." In *Provokation und Toleranz. Festschrift für Alexander Mitscherlich zum siebzigsten Geburts-tag,* 278–94. Frankfurt.

Eidelberg, L. 1934. Beiträge zum Studium des Masochismus. *Inter-nationale Zeitschrift für Psychoanalyse* 20: 330–53.

Eissler, K. R. 1977. Comments on penis envy and orgasm in women. *Psychoanalytic Study of the Child* 32: 29–32.

Engels, F. 1890. Letter to Isidor Ehrenfreund. Cited in Marx/Engels/Lenin/Stalin, *Deutsche Geschichte,* vol. 2. East Berlin, 1953.

Erikson, E. H. 1959. *Identity and the life cycle; selected papers, with a historical introd. by David Rapaport.* New York.

Fairbairn, W. R. D. 1954. *An object-relations theory of the personality.* New York.

Fenichel, O. 1940. Psychoanalysis of antisemitism. *American Imago* 1: 24–39.

———. 1945. *The psychoanalytic theory of neurosis.* New York.

———. 1953–54. *Collected papers.* New York.

Fester, R., M. König, and D. Jonas. 1979. *Weib und Macht.* Frankfurt.

Fetscher, I. 1965. Zur Entstehung des politischen Anti-semitismus in Deutschland. In *Antisemitismus,* ed. H. Huss and A. Schröder, 9–33. Frankfurt.

Figes, E. 1974. Patriarchal attitudes. Cited by C. Lasch, Freud on women. *The New York Review of Books,* October 1974.

Fraiberg, S. 1969. Libidinal object constancy and mental representation. *Psychoanalytic Study of the Child* 24: 9–47.

Freud, A. 1965. *Normality and pathology in childhood, assessments of development.* New York.

Freud, S. 1963. *The Standard Edition of the Complete Psychological Works of Sigmund Freud.* London.

———. [1905] 1963. Three essays on the theory of sexuality. *S.E.,* vol. 7.

———. [1910] 1963. A special type of object choice made by men. (Contributions to the psychology of love I). *S.E.,* vol. 11.

———. [1912; 1918] 1963. Contributions to the psychology of love. II and III. *S.E.,* vol. 11.

———. [1914] 1963. Narcissism: An introduction. *S.E.,* vol. 14.

———. [1915a] 1963. Instincts and their vicissitudes. *S.E.,* vol. 14.

———. [1915b] 1963. Repression. *S.E.,* vol. 14.

———. [1917] 1963. Mourning and melancholia. *S.E.,* vol. 14.

———. [1920] 1963. Beyond the pleasure principle. *S.E.,* vol. 18.

———. [1923] 1963. The ego and the id. *S.E.,* vol. 19.

———. [1924] 1963. The economic problem of masochism. *S.E.,* vol. 19.

———. [1925] 1963. Some psychical consequences of the anatomical distinction between the sexes. *S.E.,* vol. 19.

——. [1926] 1963. Inhibitions, symptoms and anxiety. *S.E.*, vol. 20.

——. [1930] 1963. Civilization and its discontents. *S.E.*, vol. 21.

——. [1931] 1963. Female sexuality. *S.E.*, vol. 21.

——. [1933] 1963. New introductory lectures on psycho-analysis. Lecture XXXIII. Femininity. *S.E.*, vol. 22.

——. [1939] 1963. Moses and monotheism. Three essays, *S.E.*, vol. 23.

——. 1960. *Letters, 1873–1939*. Edited by Ernst L. Freud and translated by Tania Stern and James Stern. London, 1961.

Fromm, E. 1973. *The anatomy of human destructiveness*. New York.

Galenson, E. 1976. Panel report: Psychology of women: Late adolescence and early adult. *Journal of the American Psychoanalytic Association* 24: 631–45.

Galenson, E., and H. Roiphe. 1976. Some suggested revisions concerning early female development. In *Female psychology. See* Blum 1976.

Gillespie, W. 1969. Concepts of vaginal orgasm. *International Journal of Psychoanalysis* 14: 57–70.

——. 1975. Freud's Ansichten über die weibliche Sexualität. *Psyche* 29: 789–804.

Greenacre, Ph. 1950. The prepuberty trauma in girls. *Psychoanalytic Quarterly* 19: 298–317.

——. 1971. Notes on the influence and contribution of ego psychology to the practice of psychoanalysis. In *Separation-individuation: Essays in honor of Margaret Mahler,* ed. J. B. McDevitt and C. F. Settlage. New York.

Greenson, R. R. 1954. The struggle against identification. *Journal of the American Psychoanalytic Association* 2: 200–217.

——. 1967. *The technique and practice of psychoanalysis*. London.

——. 1968. Dis-identifying from mother: Its special importance for the boy. *International Journal of Psycho-Analysis* 49: 370–74.

——. 1978. *Explorations in psychoanalysis*. New York.

Grunberger, B. 1960. Etude sur la relation objectale anale. *Revue Française de Psychanalyse* 24: 138–60, 166–68.

——. 1962. Dynamische Motive des Antisemitismus. *Psyche* 16: 255–72.

———. 1964a. Outline for a study of narcissism in female sexuality. In *Female Sexuality*. *See* Chasseguet-Smirgel 1964.

———. 1964b. Über das Phallische. *Psyche* 17: 604–20.

———. 1971. *Narcissism*. New York, 1979.

Hagemann-White, C., ed. 1979. *Frauenbewegung und Psychoanalyse*. Frankfurt.

Hartmann, H., E. Kris, and R. M. Loewenstein. 1949. Notes on the theory of aggression. *Psychoanalytic Study of the Child* 3/4: 9–36.

Hartmann, H. 1964. *Essays on ego psychology; selected problems in psychoanalytic theory*. London.

Hoffer, W. 1950. Oral aggressions and ego development. *International Journal of Psycho-Analysis* 31: 156–60.

Horney, K. 1923. The genesis of the female castration complex. In *Feminine psychology*. *See* Horney 1967.

———. 1933. The denial of the vagina. In *Feminine psychology*. *See* Horney 1967.

———. 1967. *Feminine psychology*. London.

Jacobson, E. 1937. Wege der weiblichen Über-Ich-Bildung. *Internationale Zeitschrift für Psychoanalyse* 23: 402–12.

———. 1950. Development of the wish for a child in boys. *Psychoanalytic Study of the Child* 5: 139–53.

———. 1964. *The self and the object world*. New York.

Jones, E. 1927. Child analysis. *International Journal of Psycho-Analysis* 8: 387–91.

———. 1933. The phallic phase. *Internationale Zeitschrift für Psychoanalyse* 19: 322–57. [English?]

———. 1935. The early stages of female sexual development. *Internationale Zeitschrift für Psychoanalyse* 21: 331–41.

———. 1953. *The Life and Work of Sigmund Freud*. New York, 1953.

Kestenberg, J. S. 1968. Outside and inside, male and female. *Journal of the American Psychoanalytic Association* 16: 457–520.

———. 1976. Regression and reintegration in pregnancy. In *Female psychology*. *See* Blum 1976.

Kleeman, J. A. 1976. Freud's views on early female sexuality in the light of direct child observation. In *Female psychology. See* Blum 1976.

Klein, M. 1932. *The psychoanalysis of children.* New York, 1975.

———. 1955. Neid und Dankbarkeit. *Psyche* 11: 241–55.

Klein, M. and J. Rivière. 1939. *Seelische Urkonflikte.* Munich, 1974.

Kohut, H. 1973. *The psychology of the self and the treatment of narcissism.* New York, 1985.

Kris, E. 1952. *Psychoanalytic explorations in art.* New York.

———. 1975. *Selected papers of Ernst Kris.* New Haven.

Lampl-de Groot, J. 1927. Zur Entwicklungsgeschichte des Ödipuskomplexes der Frau. *Internationale Zeitschrift für Psychoanalyse* 13.

———. 1933. Zu den Problemen der Weiblichkeit. *Internationale Zeitschrift für Psychoanalyse* 19: 385–415.

Lantos, B. 1958. Die zwei genetischen Ursprünge der Aggression und ihre Beziehungen zur Sublimierung und Neutralisierung. *Psyche* 12: 161–69.

Levinson, D. 1978. *The seasons of a man's life.* New York.

Lichtenstein, H. 1977. *The dilemma of human identity.* New York.

Loewald, H. W. 1972. Negative therapeutic reaction. *Journal of the American Psychoanalytic Association* 20: 235–45.

Loewenstein, R. M. 1951. *Christians and Jews. A Psychoanalytic Study.* New York.

Lowenfeld, H., and Y. Lowenfeld. 1970. Die permissive Gesellschaft und das Überich. *Psyche* 24: 706–20.

Mahler, M. S. 1965. On the significance of the normal separation-individuation phase: With reference to research in symbiotic child psychosis. In *Drives, affects, behavior*, ed. M. Schur, vol. 2, 161–69. New York.

———. 1968. *On human symbiosis and the vicissitudes of individuation.* New York.

———. 1972. On the first three subphases of the separation-individuation process. *International Journal of Psycho-Analysis* 53: 333–38.

Mahler, M. S., F. Pine, and A. Bermann. 1975. *The psychological birth of the human infant*. New York.

Marcuse, H. 1963. The obsolescence of the Freudian concept of man. In *Five Lectures: psychoanalysis, politics, and utopia*. Boston, 1970.

Masson, J. 1983. (Re: problems in the Sigmund Freud Archives) Cited by J. Malcolm in *The New Yorker*, December.

Masters, W. H., and V. E. Johnson. *Human Sexual Response*. St. Louis, 1966.

Mead, M. 1928. *Coming of age in Samoa. A psychological study of primitive youth for western civilization*. New York.

Menninger, K. 1938. *Man against himself*. New York.

———. 1965. *The vital balance; the life process in mental health and illness*. New York.

Miller, A. 1979. *Prisoners of childhood*. New York, 1981.

Minutes of the Vienna Psychoanalytic Society, edited by H. Nunberg and Ernst Federn and translated by M. Nunberg. New York, 1962–75.

Mitscherlich, A. 1963. *Society without the father: A contribution to social psychology*. New York, 1969.

Mitscherlich, A., et al. 1962 Symposion über "Die psychologischen und sozialen Voraussetzungen für den Antisemitismus." *Psyche* 16: 255–72.

Mitscherlich, A., and M. Mitscherlich. 1975. Das sechste Gebot. In *Die zehn Gebote heute*, 150–53. Dortmund and Munich.

Mitscherlich, A., and M. Mitscherlich. 1983. Väter und Väterlichkeit. In *Gesammelte Schriften*, ed. A. Mitscherlich, vol. 3, 371–413. Frankfurt.

Mitscherlich, M. 1971. Entwicklungsbedingte und gesellschaftsspezifische Verhaltensweisen der Frau. *Psyche* 25: 911–31.

———. 1975a. Psychoanalyse und weibliche Sexualität. *Psyche* 29: 769–88.

———. 1975b. Sittlichkeit und Kriminalität. Psychoanalytische Bemerkungen zu Karl Kraus. *Psyche* 29: 131–53.

———. 1975c. Theorien und Probleme der psychosexuellen Entwicklung der Frau. In *Therapie sexueller Störungen*, ed. V. Sigusch, 54–73. Stuttgart, New York.

——. 1977. Psychoanalytische Bemerkungen zu Franz Kafka. *Psyche* 31: 60–83.

——. 1978. Zur Psychoanalyse der Weiblichkeit. *Psyche* 32: 669–94.

Müller, J. 1931. Ein Beitrag zur Frage der Libidoentwicklung des Mädchens in der genitalen Phase. *Internationale Zeitschrift für Psychoanalyse* 17: 256–62.

Parens, H. 1979. *The development of aggression in early childhood.* New York, London.

Parin, P., F. Morgenthaler, and G. Parin-Matthèy. 1971. *Fear thy neighbor as thyself: Psychoanalysis and society among the Anyi of West Africa.* Chicago, 1980.

Person, E. 1974. Some observations on femininity. In *Women and psychoanalysis: Dialogues on psychoanalytic views of femininity*, ed. J. Strouse. New York.

Pross, H. 1979. Politische Partizipation von Frauen in der Bundesrepublik Deutschland. In *Die Psychologie des 20. Jahrhunderts*, vol. 8, pp. 503–09. Aurich.

Reich, A. 1953. Narcissistic object choice in women. *Journal of the American Psychoanalytic Association* 1: 22–44.

Reinke-Köberer, E. 1978. Zur heutigen Diskussion der weiblichen Sexualität in der psychoanalytischen Bewegung. *Psyche* 32: 695–731.

Rohde-Dachser, Ch. Ca. 1982. Frauen als Psychotherapeuten; Das Janusgesicht einer Emanzipation und die Folgen. Unpublished manuscript.

Rotmann, M. 1978. Über die Bedeutung des Vaters in der "Rapprochement-Phase." *Psyche* 32: 1105–47.

Rotter, L. 1934. Zur Psychologie der weiblichen Sexualität. *Internationale Zeitschrift für Psychoanalyse* 20: 367–74.

Schafer, R. 1968. *Aspects of internalization.* New York.

——. 1974. Problems in Freud's psychology of women. *Journal of the American Psychoanalytic Association* 22: 459–85.

Schick, P. 1965. *Karl Kraus.* Reinbek bei Hamburg.

Schottlaender, F. 1946. *Die Mutter als Schicksal.* Stuttgart.

Schupper, F. 1962. Dynamische Motive des Antisemitismus. In *Jahrbuch der Psychoanalyse*, vol. 2, pp. 3–24. Cologne and Opladen.

Schwarzer, A. 1977. (Männerhass). *Emma*, March.

Sheehy, G. 1974. *Passages: Predictable crises of adult life*. New York.

Sherfey, M. J. 1966. *The nature and evolution of female sexuality*. New York, 1972.

Shorter, E. 1975. *The making of the modern family*. New York.

———. 1982. *A history of women's bodies*. New York.

Silbermann, A. 1981. *Der ungeliebte Jude. Zur Soziologie des Antisemitismus*. Osnabrück.

Simmel, E. ed. 1964. *Anti-semitism: A social disease*. New York.

Spitz, R. A. 1957. *Nein und Ja*. Stuttgart, 1967.

———. 1965. *The First Year of Life*. New York, 1965.

———. 1976. *Vom Dialog*. Stuttgart.

Staewen-Haas, R. 1970. Identifizierung und weibliche Kastrationsangst. *Psyche* 24: 23–29.

Stoller, R. J. 1968. *Sex and gender*. New York.

———. 1974. Sex and phantasies; an examination of Freud's concept of bisexuality. In *Women and psychoanalysis*, ed. J. Strouse. New York.

———. 1975. *Perversion. The erotic form of hatred*. New York.

———. 1979. *Sexual excitement: Dynamics of erotic life*. New York.

Strindberg, A. 1884–86. *The father*. In *Strindberg, Five Plays*. Translated, with an introduction, by Harry G. Carlson. Berkeley, 1983.

———. 1884–86. *Die Verheirateten*.

Sullivan, H. S. 1953. *The interpersonal theory of psychiatry*. New York.

Taylor, H. 1851. On the enfranchisement of women. In *Essays on sex equality, by John Stuart Mill and Harriet Taylor Mill*, ed. Alice S. Rossi. Chicago, 1970.

Thomä, H. 1967. Konversionshysterie und weiblicher Kastrationskomplex. *Psyche* 21: 139–55.

Ticho, G. R. 1976. Female autonomy and young adult women. In *Female psychology. See* Blum 1976.

Tolpin, M. 1971. On the beginning of a cohesive self. *Psychoanalytic Study of the Child* 26: 316–52.

Torok, M. 1964. The significance of penis envy in women. In *Female sexuality. See* Chasseguet-Smirgel 1964.

Vilar, E. 1971. *The manipulated man.* London, 1972.

Wangh, M. 1962. Psychologische Betrachtungen zur Dynamik und Genese des Vorurteils, des Antisemitismus und des Nazismus. *Psyche* 16: 273–84.

——Winnicott, D. W. 1965a. *The family and individual development.* London, 1966.

——. 1965b. *The maturational processes and the facilitating environment; studies in the theory of emotional development.* London.

——. 1971. *Playing and reality.* London.

Wolf, Ch. 1976. *A model childhood.* Translated by Ursule Molinaro and Hedwig Rappolt. New York, 1980.

Wolfenstein, M. 1951. A phase in the development of children's sense of humor. *Psychoanalytic Study of the Child* 6: 336–50.

Zilboorg, G. 1944. Männlich und weiblich. In *Frauenbewegung und Psychoanalyse. See* C. Hagemann-White 1979.

Index